WHO GIVES A POOP?

Also by Heather L. Montgomery

Something Rotten

Bugs Don't Hug

Little Monsters

How Rude!

Wild Discoveries

WHO GIVES A POOP?

SURPRISING SCIENCE FROM ONE END TO THE OTHER

Heather L. Montgomery
ILLUSTRATED BY **Iris Gottlieb**

BLOOMSBURY
CHILDREN'S BOOKS
NEW YORK LONDON OXFORD NEW DELHI SYDNEY

Library of Congress Cataloging-in-Publication Data
Names: Montgomery, Heather L., author. | Gottlieb, Iris, illustrator.
Title: Who gives a poop? / by Heather L. Montgomery ; illustrated by Iris Gottlieb.
Description: New York : Bloomsbury, 2020.
Summary: The author explores various scientific and medical applications of poop.
Identifiers: LCCN 2020020258 (print) | LCCN 2020020259 (e-book)
ISBN 978-1-5476-0347-3 (hardcover) • ISBN 978-1-5476-0348-0 (e-book)
Subjects: LCSH: Feces—Juvenile literature. | Animal droppings—Juvenile literature.
Classification: LCC QP159 .M66 2020 (print) | LCC QP159 (e-book) | DDC 612.3/6—dc23
LC record available at https://lccn.loc.gov/2020020258
LC e-book record available at https://lccn.loc.gov/2020020259

Book design by Jeanette Levy
Typeset by Westchester Publishing Services
Printed and bound in the U.S.A. by Berryville Graphics Inc., Berryville, Virginia
2 4 6 8 10 9 7 5 3 1

To find out more about our authors and books visit
www.bloomsbury.com and sign up for our newsletters.

Dedicated to every person who has stick-stirred some scat

CONTENTS

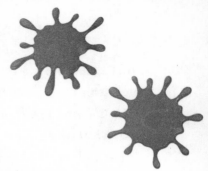

CHAPTER 1
HUNK OF TONGUE

The air was brisk, the trucks were loud, and I had a hunk of tongue tucked into my pocket.

I was happy.

Well, *not* happy about the mangled legs, trail of guts, and cold coyote heart that lay in front of me just a few yards from the interstate.

That coyote—with a ruff at her neck as lush as my kitty's and a tail as bushy as my pup's—must have had a run-in with a car and would never howl again.[1] The thought could have derailed me, but thanks to earlier research, I knew Dr. Bridgett vonHoldt at Princeton University was waiting to hear this howler's story: where had she come from, who were her kin, what could we learn from the secret code inside her cells? So, I had slapped on some gloves, snipped a bit of tongue, packed it into a vial, and placed it safely in my pocket.[2] I felt some satisfaction.

---

[1] It was so chewed up I couldn't truly tell the sex, but there was another road-killed coyote less than a mile down the road that was all boy, so I'm guessing this was his mate.

[2] Yes, I carry a tongue-collecting kit in my car: snippy scissors, silicon beads for preservation, and cute little vials with tight caps.

Just imagine, there in my pocket sat microscopic strands of DNA code—a twisted ribbon of A's, T's, C's, and G's that spell out instructions for every paw, claw, nail, or tail on this planet.[3]

Inherited from her mama and papa, those alphabetical strands could answer my questions—well, really, Dr. vonHoldt's questions—about how coyotes have moved across the eastern US.[4] As I rose to return to my car, though, something wiggled in the back of my brain. Once I slipped those slimy bits into the vials and shipped them off, I'd lose touch with this creature. Her data would be locked down in a digital database, a cold, hard place where numbers get crunched. Sure, her data (info) would be valued, but my connection to her would be severed. Walking back to my car, I wanted to know more. Where did she go last night? Who did she howl with? What moonlit canyons did she haunt?

I wasn't ready to let her go.

Sidestepping a pile of poop, I almost toppled down the slope. But wait. Those weren't the smooth, solid sausages my pup, Piper, excretes. There was something there. Some clue that had me scrambling back up, leaning in, grabbing—yes, yes, you safety

---

[3] DNA is made of 4 different building blocks, each with a different base: **a**denine, **t**hymine, **c**ytosine, or **g**uanine.

[4] I learned Dr. vonHoldt's story when I was writing *Something Rotten: A Fresh Look at Roadkill*. She studies canine ancestry (ance**story**?) and is particularly interested in genetic admixture: when previously separated groups of animals begin breeding with each other, their DNA gets blended. A while back, coyotes from the western US hopped the Mississippi River and started mixing and mingling with eastern wolves. The DNA of their pups tells that tale. It also leads to lots of questions: Who's a wolf? Who's a coyote? What's the difference? Does it even matter?

police, I still had my gloves on. You don't think I fish around in coyote slop without my handy-dandy latex gloves, do you?

The chunks, glossy enough to reflect the October sky, sported chestnut-brown seeds. I hefted a hunk in my hand. The turd was as wide as a quarter, and wiggly white hairs sprang out from the brown gunk. This was no pet poo.

This, I suspected, was the last story the living coyote ever had the chance to tell.

As stinky as it was, I couldn't ignore *that* story.

My eyes read the obvious stuff: seeds = ate fruit. My finger and thumb mashed through it and registered something gristly and grotesque: one pea-sized paw = ate meat.[5] My brain swiped through my mental files: hair = ate mammal. My nose sniff-sniffed: stink = ??? What did that blur of odors mean? I longed for the nasal capacity of a canid.[6]

So, there I stood beside that interstate, this pile in front of me loaded with information I could not access, odors I could not isolate, treasures I could not cash in. Trained as a biologist, with years working as a naturalist, I've got plenty of experience squatting, stick in hand, over animal scat. But in all that stirring, rarely had I come up with solid answers. I knew, just *knew*, there had to be someone out there who could really read a clue from poo. That's the kind of thinking that led me to spend a few years with my nose down, poking at poop.

---

[5] A coyote gulps small prey whole, claws and all. Who has a pea-sized paw? A lizard, a mouse, a chipmunk? Although it was mangled, Toe 1 (the thumb) was set off to the side and Toe 3 was longer than the rest, so I'm guessing a shrew, an insect-gulping mammal that looks like a mouse with a long snout.

[6] Recently an olfaction specialist (smell expert) claimed that human olfaction is just as good as dogs. So maybe what I needed was more practice.

Okay, I'll admit it: I've always been partial to poop. One of my favorite smells is horse manure. Weird, right? But every time I inhale that grassy goodness, I'm instantly back at horse camp, a velvety muzzle tickling my cheek. I want that connection with every creature.

What if every time I stepped up to scat, I could feel as if I were beside that bear, bobcat, or beetle hunched and helpless at a moment of vulnerability, pausing to make a deposit?

And, what, in the end, is an animal actually depositing? As I dug into this topic, I discovered mounds more than leftover food. Like a trip down the slippery slide of a digestive tract, questions took me into kinks and curves, places I never would have expected—or ever thought I wanted to go.

Once I put my poo goggles on, I found fecal fun everywhere. Like at the Hawaiian beach where the sand you sift through your fingers might be parrotfish poop.[7] Like the ghastly gorilla toe I saw sitting in leopard poop.[8] Like the bear scientist whose hands were so busy cradling a cub she had to pop a poop sample into her mouth.[9] And take this story of a South American scorpion: If a predator has the scorpion by the tail, it's no problem. The scorpion self-amputates his tail and skitters away. The problem? He loses

---

[7] The fish chomp on coral reefs and then, well, you know ... A single flashy fish can produce 1,000 pounds of sand a year.

[8] Um, how did that not get digested? And who knew that leopards eat gorillas?!

[9] Better hope that baggie has a good seal!

his hind end and can't regrow it. The sad scorpion is now missing his number one weapon, but his bigger problem may be number two. His rear end heals over—with no hole! Then his doo-doo has nowhere to go-go. For the rest of his life, he has to hold it.[10]

So, on this slippery trip, most of the curves had my stomach flipping with fun, but along with all that potty humor and serious science, some of the swerves stirred up black bile. I'd be tunneling along into the guts of some study, hot on the tail of an opossum or tale of an orangutan, then a kink would kick me off into an appendix. A dead end. A black hole—a place where dark questions lurk—questions that led me to question my very understanding of "right."

But there's plenty of time for stewing and brewing in dark matter later. For now, come join my romp through giggly guts and terrific turds. To launch our journey, all you have to do is be willing to dig in![11]

---

[10]This happens more often to males—no one knows why. What happens to his poo? It packs in his gut like wadded-up cotton. One scorpion self-amputated a second time—with no predators around. White stuff squirted out. Was he sacrificing segments just to take a dump?

[11] But let me do the dirty work. Touching feces, stirring feces, sniffing feces—all risky enough that you need to be properly trained and protected before you *actually* dig in.

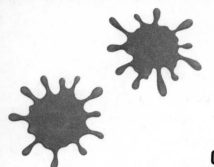

CHAPTER 2
POOPY PUZZLE

In the dark of the night, my tires splashed through thick mud puddles. My headlights lit tall tree trunks, and my car eased across a creaky covered bridge. I was headed deep into a forest in south Alabama, a place where longleaf pine trees wave foot-long needles high above and gopher tortoises crawl through 50-foot tunnels far below.[1] There, wildlife trackers from across the country were gathered to see what they could read from the sign left on the landscape. Not road signs or park signs, but "wildlife sign"—like fur caught on a twig, a chew mark on a nut, or a stinky scat—that could have similar meanings.

Hannah could look at a blob that swirled and curled and tell that a turkey was a hen (female) because gobbler scat is shaped like a J. Dustin told stories of hunters tasting deer droppings. We all knew that was a bad idea.[2] If it's bitter, Dustin said, the deer had been eating acorns, and the hunters would head to the nearest oak

---

[1] An entire ecosystem counts on gopher tortoise tunnels for safe shelter when forest fires flare. More than 350 species depend on these tortoises, including a beetle that refuses to eat anything except gopher tortoise droppings.
[2] *Not* wise. Besides being gross, deer carry zoonotic diseases—ones that can spread to humans—like giardia, which will give you gravy in your britches.

grove. And then there was our leader, Casey. Casey who described wildlife sign as "beautiful expressions of different tribes of animals." Casey who would look at bark scraped from a sapling and then let his body become the buck—his torso angled, hands held like hooves in midprance, his head regal under the weight of imagined antlers.[3] Casey who had once pulled a 3-foot tapeworm right up from a mass of bear scat.

"Sign is the thing," he told me. Tracks demonstrate "how an animal interacts with the planet. But the sign is what really expresses their particular ecological relationship." Finding sign, he said as his brown eyes went dreamy, is far more intimate.

And what is the most intimate of animal sign? To me, that was all about scat.

You might not think that Alabama is the place to go for finding scat from dreamy creatures. Sure, it's not the Arctic, the Amazon, or the Himalayas, but Alabama's got cool critters, too.[4] Under a bridge that weekend I scooped up some bat scat (better known as guano) and hauled it home. Time to get intimate.

✓ Microscope[5]
✓ Jeweler's loupe (a magnifying glass you can hold in your eye)

---

[3] Antlers can grow up to 4 cm a day. To do that, they steal calcium from the bucks' ribs, which go osteoporotic—weak from a loss of calcium. Researchers want to know how deer build their bones back up. Maybe we could steal that idea to help humans with osteoporosis.

[4] Alabama has more species of freshwater fish, crayfish, snails, mussels, turtles, and carnivorous plants than any other state—and it's tiny compared to giants like Texas and California!

[5] The first scope I remember using was in seventh grade. Peering into that eyepiece at creatures invisible to everyone else, at the stuff that made up my cheek, at the stacked cells that keep a mighty redwood standing—that day, the universe began to make sense.

✓ Paper bags
✓ Gloves, mask, goggles
✓ Probe, forceps, scalpel

All my gear was laid out on my dining room table. Okay, not directly on the table. Sorry, plastic tablecloth, no more picnics for you. There were personal shields at work, too. The goggles cut into my face, the mask got hot and nasty, and the gloves gave my hands a funky smell, but those were all minor inconveniences compared to the needles that would be jabbed into my skin if I got rabies, the medical tests I'd face if I caught a lung fungus, or the pain I'd suffer from any other disease bats get blamed for.[6]

The bat turd was the size of a cooked grain of white rice, but it was black. Through the lens of the loupe it sparkled.[7] Sliding it under the more powerful lens of my microscope, I discovered why: It was a junkyard of bug parts. Each piece a different texture—ridged, sharp, dimpled—but almost all were shiny.

My eyes flitted around the binocular eyepieces. In college I spent a whole semester looking at insects under a scope, but those parts had been hooked together on the bug. I'd never seen anything like this. It was like looking around an antique store and knowing the thing hanging on the wall is a tool but not quite being able to figure out what it does. Is that an insect's jaw? Could that be a knee? That claw came from a bug? What is that fleck of cream-colored foam?[8] Under the pressure of my scalpel blade, the log of

---

[6] The rabies virus hangs out in spit glands, so it is usually spread by bites, but it can be inhaled if small bits get lifted into the air. All the more reason you shouldn't try this at home.

[7] Polar bear poo sparkles, too, sometimes. When a zookeeper needs to know who's who among the poo, they sprinkle different colors of glitter into each bear's dinner.

[8] In addition to shooting light from below to see inside the sample (like a compound microscope does), my scope could also shoot light from above to see the outside.

8

guano crumbled. Black bits scattered across a white dessert plate.[9]

Brown, yellow, black, translucent. Then there was 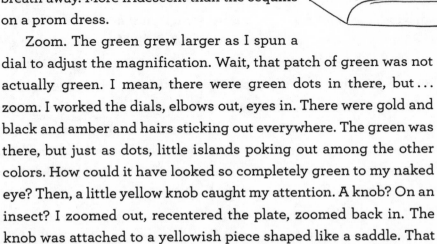 the green. A shimmery green that took my breath away. More iridescent than the sequins on a prom dress.

Zoom. The green grew larger as I spun a dial to adjust the magnification. Wait, that patch of green was not actually green. I mean, there were green dots in there, but... zoom. I worked the dials, elbows out, eyes in. There were gold and black and amber and hairs sticking out everywhere. The green was there, but just as dots, little islands poking out among the other colors. How could it have looked so completely green to my naked eye? Then, a little yellow knob caught my attention. A knob? On an insect? I zoomed out, recentered the plate, zoomed back in. The knob was attached to a yellowish piece shaped like a saddle. That could be the outside of a bug's body, but it didn't explain the knob.

I aimed my probe and my forceps at it. I needed to see the other side.

Pling.

At the touch of the probe, the knob tiddlywinked out of view.

No!

I pulled my eyes from the viewers. Where did it go? There, in the white space just below the decorative edge of the plate, sat a black fleck.

Maybe?

Slide. Zoom. Slide. Zoom. There.

---

[9] What would Grandma say? But, hey, the plate fit nicely under the microscope's stage.

Yes!

The piece had landed upside down. I looked into the knob and saw what looked like rows and rows of tiny windows. The top was completely covered in small prisms. This, I realized, is part of a face. I was looking at the world through the eye of an insect! Now, that's a new perspective.[10]

For an hour my eyes bounced around in that miniature playground. Something triangular, something antler-like, lots of oddball parts that led me toward knowing the bat on a whole new level, but who did those parts come from? I worked to put the pieces together, but when the colors matched, the edges didn't. When the textures went together, the shapes didn't fit. How many pieces was I missing? It was like working a jigsaw puzzle, but instead of one puzzle, it was piles of puzzles swirled together. No instructions, no pretty picture on a puzzle box, and no clue how many insects were jumbled together in there.

Into the afternoon I hunched over the scope, my scalpel and forceps scurried and scavenged. It was as impossible as building a roller coaster from the stuff in a junk drawer. Hours later, my eyes blurry, my neck screaming, I gave up.

How does anyone ever make meaning from a hodgepodge of poopy parts?[11]

---

[10] An insect's compound eye is made of many separate units called ommatidia. Each ommatidium has its own lens. A fruit fly may have 700. A dragonfly, 30,000. I think this eye belonged to a beetle.

[11] Meaning isn't the only thing people make from poo. In Maine, an artist makes poo-poo clocks that mark 1-turdy, 2-turdy, 3-turdy. In Australia, an engineer is making bricks from human poo (imagine that bedroom wall). And in Russia, a researcher dreamed up a way for soldiers trapped in a tank to dispose of their solid waste—pack it in a shell and use it as ammo!

CHAPTER 3
POO-POO CHOO-CHOO

I was reading a book about how dogs were first domesticated, when something just about jumped off the page. In a cave in Texas, they found human feces that were 9,400 years old. In those feces, they found a dog's bone. A bone from inside a dog's body, not from inside a dog's toy box. The book plopped down onto my knees. This meant ... a person ate a dog.

My dog, Piper, snored on the floor beside me. I swallowed hard, trying to settle something that squiggled in my gut.

I never meant to look at human poop. It is just too ...

Sure, I check my own to make sure everything is working properly, but looking at other people's? Too personal, too private, too revealing ... maybe too gross, even for me.

Then on Twitter, a photo of smiling LEGO heads caught my eye. Six medical professionals had a question: When a human swallows a foreign object, how long does it take to pass? Their instruments: LEGO heads, their own digestive tracts, and chopsticks/tongue depressors/whatever else was handy and disposable. Their scientific procedure: Swallow one head, poke through their own poo for days, and hopefully discover a yellow smilie staring back at them.[1] Their results: the average FART (Found and Retrieval Time) is 1.7 days. Their conclusion: Parents, when your kid swallows a LEGO, chill out. It'll all come out okay.

People retweeted. They called the researchers legends, said they should win the Ig Nobel prize,[2] and they wished the LEGO heads could tell their side of the story.

When you put that kind of spin on it, it's hard to resist that story, even if it is human poo.

Medical research normally requires years of slow stuff (making sure the test is safe, getting permission to test on animals, doing pilot tests on rats, and finally getting to test humans). Then, you get results and wait to get it published. Once it is out there in the world, you wait again for someone to read it, care about it, and maybe, just maybe, pass it along to someone who needs it. On average, that process takes 17 years; thanks to social media (and their whole humorous approach), this story spread in just a few days.

I ran across another human poo story that went viral, too. That one had me chasing it down a winding road in central Alabama.

The tires whined across the asphalt of the little country lane in the middle of nowhere. I barreled over a hill, then slammed on the brakes and threw the car in reverse.[3] That "hill" was a bridge over the train tracks I was seeking.

---

[1] One participant never found his. Did he just miss it? Or will it pop out in 10 years?
[2] The perfect parody of the Nobel Prize. The Improbable Research website states, "The Ig Nobel Prize honors achievements that make people LAUGH, and then THINK."
[3] Hey, this is Alabama. We can do that.

When my car reached the top, I lowered the window, poked my head out, and pulled in a long breath.

Nothing.

Well, it was April in Alabama, so there was plenty of pollen and a hint of tar from the train tracks below. But that was not what I had trekked across the state to sniff out.

I was on the hunt for the poop train—56 train cars filled with feces.

And I wasn't the only one. NBC, CNN, NPR, *The Wall Street Journal*—everybody wanted to know about the sleepy little town called Parrish and the 10 million pounds of poop sitting in its rail yard.

Where did all of it come from? Where was it all going? What did that *look* like? What did that *smell* like? Five minutes before I reached the town, I sniffed again. Nothing. At the stop light, nothing.

Hmmm. I hadn't bothered to track down exactly where the train was before I had jumped into the car. Parrish has only 982 residents; it's only 2 miles across. I was counting on smell to lead me to it.

The really nice thing about really small southern towns is that the folks are really helpful. With a flick of his ball cap, the guy at the gas station sent me down the street to the city hall. The clerk there didn't know the street name, but she rounded up two folks who did. Pretty soon I was turning down a lane dotted with the friendly flowers of dogwood trees. On my right was a house trailer with a basketball hoop in the yard, and on my left was a rail yard with 30-some boxes in the yard. Metal boxes, like the ones you see on tractor trailers. This had to be the right train. It looked just like the pictures in all the news articles: gray rusting boxes with the word *EPIC* printed boldly on their sides, stacked 2 high.

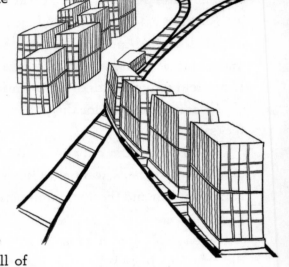

I swung my car onto the grass on the left side of the road. Now, I had been excited by the idea of the train's odor, but looking at all those boxes, I wondered if maybe this wasn't such a good idea. Can you imagine what even one train car full of feces would smell like? I sat for a moment with the windows shut tight, gathering my grit. I had to do it, though. I had to know. So, I swung open the door, and . . .

Not really much at all, actually.

There was a slight tang in the air like a sour wet rag. It was a brisk 50°F and had rained last night. There was also a musty kind of undercurrent like a dark draft drifting up from a basement, but nothing nearly as bad as I expected.

I peered through a patch of weeds and trees at the rail yard. It was long and narrow with 5 sets of tracks side by side and a long parking lot crowded with trucks and equipment. On the far end, there was action. A large contraption, like a forklift on steroids, had big yellow arms stretched out in front. It drove toward the railroad tracks. I started snapping pictures. Then, the driver got out and swaggered my way.

Wait, was I doing something wrong? My car was parked on the edge of the road, on the public right-of-way; I wasn't standing in anyone's yard. My eyes darted around for No Trespassing signs. I leaped into the car and revved the engine. The man stopped at the edge of the tracks, pulled out his own phone, and started snapping pics in my direction. Was I in trouble? Had he gotten a picture of my license plate?

As I pulled away, I spotted a gentleman bent over some plants in his yard down a side street. A witness, I thought. A local person who lives right here. What is it like for him, living beside all that? Ray Madison wasn't afraid to tell me what it had been like.

"Yesterday," Mr. Madison said, "it was horrible. Ooooh. Oooooweee! The wind was blowing ... It just stunk like you were in a busted septic area." He waved his arm at the homes in his quiet neighborhood. "The only thing [is, it] cooled down today. If it never rained, you would have smelt it."

The wind, I realized, was blowing the smell away from us.

"I have my vegetable garden right here every year," he said with a slow shake of his head. I eyed plant pots waiting beside a bare square of soil. Soil I imagined should soon be bursting with sweet corn, greens, and juicy tomatoes. Would Mr. Madison dare plant anything this year?

"This is awful. You know this is unhealthy," he said.

Would you like to have *that* in your backyard?

Mr. Madison went on to tell me about the mayor's action at a town meeting. "She permitted them 3 weeks, not 3 weeks and a minute, not 3 weeks and an hour. A MONTH AND A HALF [later] and they still ..." He waved his arm off at the train cars.

That reminded me I had an appointment with the mayor, so I

took my leave and headed back to town hall to meet Heather Hall, who helped me piece together who exactly "they" were.

The containers had been headed to a landfill out in Jefferson County. The poop was supposed to be offloaded in the town of West Jefferson and then shipped the rest of the way by tractor trailer. But the people of West Jefferson were tired of holding their noses and took to the courts to prevent the poo from parading through their town.[4]

With too much poo and no place to put it, the railroad company backed the train up to a nearby rail yard, to a place where there were no lawsuits or zoning or regulation, to the tiny town of Parrish.

That was January.

"They kept coming and coming," Mayor Hall said. The landfill company didn't have permission to unload the cars in Parrish, so they just sat. "We had no idea what it was," she said, but one February day, a heat wave hit. The thermometer skyrocketed into the 80s. "With 252 containers of that stuff, it smelled like there was death everywhere in Parrish. It doesn't smell like sewage, it smells like carcasses."[5]

The people of Parrish wanted it out. Mayor Hall reached out to her senators; she begged for help. Nothing. She called an emergency council meeting. Should they grant the company a business license so they could unload the train? The vote: no way!

"If we grant them the business license, then we are stuck."

Through red-rimmed glasses Heather Hall looked me in the eye and said, "We were told it was Grade A biosolids—"

---

[4] Mayor Hall told me it took West Jefferson nearly a year to get rid of it.
[5] I had read about 56 train cars; I had seen 30-some metal containers; I had no idea that at one time there were 252 poop-filled containers parked in Parrish.

Brrrrrrp! Her intercom buzzed.

A man's voice: "Mayor?"

"Yes?"

"*Newsweek* lady."

Mayor Hall took the phone number of the *Newsweek* reporter so she could finish telling me her story.[6]

"We come to find out it is Grade A *and* Grade B, which, Grade B has pathogens and diseases and stuff." She draws a map showing how the railroad runs right along the ball fields and less than a quarter of a mile from the school. "What happens when there's heat applied to a pathogen? They grow, right? Okay, so this stuff attracts flies. You know flies. They are going to land on food."

I think of Ray Madison's tomatoes.

"What happens if somebody touches or eats something that a fly was on, that was in *that* material? How is that not a public problem?

"I talked to the EPA, talked to ADEM,[7] nothing, nothing!

"And then you have big New York City—yeah this stuff is from New York City."

Just think of that. Sewage sludge packed up on train cars and hauled 1,000 miles from New York (and New Jersey) all the way to Alabama.

Why?

---

[6] One day, students had some questions about the train. They called up Mayor Hall. She stopped everything and held a mock town meeting with them. Now, that's my kind of mayor!

[7] EPA = Environmental Protection Agency. ADEM = Alabama Department of Environmental Management.

Every day, New Yorkers flush ~1,200[8] tons of sewage. Where are you going to dump that? They used to pipe it into the ocean. The Ocean Dumping Ban of 1988 put a wrench in that. They used to ship it to landfills in Pennsylvania. The folks in PA threw a kink in that. So now the cheapest option is to send it far, far away to communities in need of any kind of income. But Parrish wasn't even getting that income.

By the time I left Mayor Hall's office, I was steamed.

You have a giant city with ~8.6 million people. A giant railroad corporation with $2.2 billion in payroll. A giant landfill with over 1,525 acres[9] waiting to be filled. And facing that wall of giants? The teeny tiny Town of Parrish.

Heather Hall must have felt pretty small.

How was anyone supposed to fight those giants? Worry lines etched across her face. How could anyone shoulder 10 million pounds of sewage sludge?

Slam! My car door got the brunt of my frustration.

A sign on the side of the road read:

Town of
PARRISH
WE LOVE OUR COAL MINERS

The story stabbed a little closer to home—both of my granddads were coal miners. These are hardworking people. People who bend their backs, spill their sweat, and fill their lungs with coal dust—all so we can have electricity. How dare we dump this on them!

---

[8] ~1,200 means about 1,200. Nobody's standing out there with a scale, so scientists have to estimate.

[9] 1,525 acres = 24,400 tennis courts' worth of land.

By the time my wheels were spitting gravel on the far edge of town, I was angry.

Of course, New York has run out of room for the poo. And that's just one city. One city flushing tons and tons of feces every day. What about the 38,000 other cities in the US? What about the other 195 countries on the planet? What about the places where flushing isn't even possible?

According to a report from the World Health Organization, 673 million people practiced open defecation in 2017.[10] How, in the twenty-first century, can there be so many people who have no option but to poop on the ground?

When human poop lies in the dirt, all those germs run free. Turn your time machine back into history: Cholera? Polio? Typhoid? All spread through germy feces. All pandemics that sliced through human life. A single cholera pandemic killed more than 800,000 people in India alone.[11] In the past 200 years, 7 cholera pandemics have swept the globe.

Maybe you've felt the effects of poopy germs yourself, thanks to a food-poisoning friend that hitched a ride from feces to lettuce then into your intestines. And don't forget parasites like tapeworms, hookworms, or flatworm flukes that swim around in feces, too.

Each day on this planet, diarrhea kills 2,195 children. Death caused by doo-doo may be one of the greatest challenges to human health, which I really don't get: why haven't people figured out a better way to deal with their poo?

---

[10] That number is twice the population of the entire United States!

[11] To put that in context, a huge football stadium holds only ~100,000 people.

Animals have. A few things they do with poo:

- Recycle: Roly polies eat their poop to recycle crucial copper.[12]
- Cool off: Shoe-billed storks drip their droppings down their legs to cool off.
- Suit of armor: The larvae of a leaf beetle wears his poop as a shield. What bird wants to bite through that?
- Communicate: Chimps fling their feces, which makes it pretty obvious when they are mad.
- Makeup: Egyptian vultures chow down on cow, sheep, or goat dung to gain yellow pigments. Bright yellow faces make the fluffy white vultures look sharp.
- Cash in: A tree shrew sits on the toilet-shaped lips of a pitcher plant and slurps up sweet nectar. All the plant asks for in return is a deposit packed with poop nutrients.
- Dig in: Dung beetles eat it, of course, but so do bunnies, butterflies, beavers, and even baby koalas, pandas, and hippos. Yum-yum!

And then there's that whole other category of how animal poo helps plants. A gossamer gob of yellow bounces through the air and perches on the telephone line near my house. That goldfinch drips a gift into the soil. Fertilizer? You bet. But maybe also a seed.

---

[12] Roly poly blood uses copper to tote oxygen through the body. When there's plenty of oxygen, the blood can turn blue!

From where? How far? What mystery tree might sprout? You can be all formal and call it seed dispersal, but to me, it is a gift from the gut. Thank you, winged one.

And where a bird may eat 76 berries from a plant, a grizzly bear can swallow 350 to 400 seeds in a single gulp. Move on up to a mighty mastodon and imagine how many seeds that megamuncher could swallow, then sow.

Okay, none of these animals sits on the john, contemplating it, but they all do put poo to good use. Nature never wastes anything.

Humans do.

Again, I don't get this. Each and every one of us has 3 pounds of awesome encased in our skull.[13] We have 100 billion neurons zip-zapping information around faster than any computer and complex enough to plan a trip to Mars, yet we waste something nature never would. Why aren't we putting our gray matter to good use on brown matter? Why aren't our brains brimming with answers to the question that is burning me up:

What else could we be doing with poo?

---

[13] 3 pounds of brain matter, equal to about 3.5 days' worth of human poop.

CHAPTER 4
DOGGIES AND DUNG

Daniella drew a long blade from a bloodred sheath. "This is like a machete," she said. "The men have it on their belt like this." She placed her hands on her hip where people carry their cell phones. Then she pointed to a 2-foot stick with a fist-sized knob at the tip. "And this is their bludgeoner."

"Oh, my." You could conk a viper with that.

We weren't in danger of stepping on a viper. We were in Daniella's apartment in the city of Birmingham, Alabama, but I felt as if I had plopped down in the African savanna. The walls were covered with carved wooden masks, machetes, and paintings of women draped in vibrant fabric and carrying water jugs on their heads. On one wall sat a canvas with an odd blue splotch. The splotch reminded me of the cross section of a brain or maybe a sponge painting, but I should have known better.

That splotch was a print from a pachyderm pad.[1]

Dr. Daniella Chusyd is kind of obsessed with elephants. She

---

[1] Art isn't the only thing elephants make. Their dung is turned into profitable paper, which helps rural communities and saves trees.

told me about the day she fell in love with them as she watched one family: "A bunch of them stopped in the middle of the river and seemed to really enjoy life at that moment, you know what I mean? You could just see it on their faces."

Daniella's concerned about the way elephant numbers are dropping. To get a better understanding, she's going to study why some elephant mamas aren't having babies. I've come to visit her to learn all about her scientific methods.

A few minutes earlier, right on her dining room table,[2] Daniella had dipped her fingers into elephant dung and parsed it out into little plastic containers. Then, she popped on caps. Each cap had 5 small holes, making it look like a saltshaker—with an altogether different spice.

Next she placed each container and a little bit of chicken into an open shoebox on the floor of her apartment. One beside the coffee table, one behind the couch, one in the kitchen, but, oddly enough, none in the bathroom. Soon, it would be time for the action.

A few barks and claws *click-clicking* told us someone else was eager to start. Daniella's sporty shoes sprinted her up the stairs and then back down with her copper-colored pup, Bennet, in tow.

"Google, Bennet, Google!" Bennet is young. The dog has only had one training session so far, but she's already picked up on Daniella's code word for "search."[3]

The dog's silky ears flop as she plows her snout into the

---

[2] See, I'm not the only one who uses her dining room as a lab table.

[3] Yep, Daniella used the name of the search engine as her search term. Can I say a word about my friend Google (and Wikipedia and every other internet option out there)? When curiosity drives me to devour more information, these friends can be an awesome place to start, but just like human friends, sometimes they lead me astray. Just like Bennet, I need to be cautious about what I put my nose into.

first box, *slurp-slurps*, and bounds off to find a second. There are 7 boxes, but only 4 contain shakers of dung and chicken treats. To reap the chicken reward, Bennet has to pick the right box. She's smart and quickly learns to snoop for the poop.

Daniella is training Bennet as a scientific instrument. Next year they will head to Africa to collect dung from forest elephants.[4] Why do you need a dog to track those megamammals? Unlike savanna elephants, who lumber across wide-open spaces, forest elephants wind their way under lush, leafy trees; you can't spy on them from a helicopter. And hacking your way through there with that machete-like blade? Not fun. So, Daniella has recruited her dogs, Moja and Bennet. There's an added benefit: their noses know if feces are fresh. Daniella's not interested in stale stuff.

But where in Alabama can she get fresh elephant dung? At 8:30 a.m. every Saturday, Daniella meets a zookeeper to get the goods. So fresh it might still be warm.[5]

While playing poop hide-and-seek with a dog might seem like fun and games, Daniella has a serious concern. "It appears that forest elephants are having babies later in life, by like a full decade, compared to savanna elephants and Asian elephants." Is this

---

[4] African elephants are split into two subspecies: forest and savanna (or bush) elephants. Daniella and many other scientists think there is enough evidence for them to be considered separate species.

[5] That zoo has a whole dumpster of dung. Want to go diving in that?

normal? Is it related to their diet? Is it because of stress? Daniella wants to know.

If you nab fresh dung, you can sneak a peek at both the animal's diet and hormones,[6] substances from inside the body that can be used to tell who's pregnant and who's not and how stressed the elephants are.

She'll be looking for metabolites, which are the leftovers from the hormones. Say you accidently step on a viper. Your glands are going to pump out hormones like adrenaline and cortisol to tell your body to get into high gear. Later, when you're safely swinging in your hammock, your body has got to get rid of those metabolized hormones, so you dump them out in your dung.[7]

Out there in the forest elephants' habitat, trees are being cut down, oil drilling is ramping up. Is being closer to humans stressing out the would-be elephant mamas? Are compounds from the plants they eat messing with their ability to absorb protein?[8] Or, is this slow reproduction perfectly normal for elephants who dine in the forest, where food might not be as nutritious as out on the savanna? Daniella aims to find out.

Between 2000 and 2011, the population of forest elephants dropped by 62 percent. What if their numbers keep cascading down? If each mama is stressed out, eating poorly, or even twiddling her

---

[6] Hormones are bossy little messengers made by glands and moved through the body by blood. Hungry? Sleepy? Stressed out? Blame a hormone.

[7] Metabolites are pure gold for zookeepers. If you use a cheetah in an animal show, how do you know if he's got stage fright? Metabolites. If you add a new gorilla to a group of teenage gorillas, how do you know if they are cool with that? Metabolites.

[8] Plants produce tannins to ward off plant eaters. Chomp into a bitter acorn and you will feel the tannin grab the proteins in your mucous membranes and draw your mouth into a pucker.

thumbs[9] for an extra 10 years before giving birth, there's going to be fewer trunks trotting around. Every bit of information Daniella collects will add to our perspective on forest elephants. Are they in fact a separate species? Are human actions changing their birth rate? Is there anything we can do to save them? This poop sleuthing is serious stuff.

One day I was scrolling through a website Daniella had mentioned when a headline caught my eye: "Poachers versus Poop." Each year up to 40,000 African elephants are axed so people can have tusks. Tusks that hang on walls as trophies or are ground into buttons, billiard balls, or bagpipe parts.[10] A photo of 100+ curved tusks lined up in a parking lot wrenched my heart. My mind flashed back to that elephant family Daniella had fallen in love with. She saw the joy on their faces. I had never *thought* about elephant emotions, but staring at the empty ends of those tusks in that photo, I *felt* elephant emotions.[11] My chest thumped for the families and their hollow hearts. Elephants deserve better. Ivory has a pretty strong draw[12]—so strong that people are willing to kill elephants, hack off their tusks, and ship them across the world. Sometimes lucky law enforcement comes across a whole shipment of ivory. Then, those smugglers will be paying their dues. That ivory won't be turned

---

[9] Okay, you're right, elephants don't have thumbs. When baby elephants need something to suck on, they suck on their trunks.

[10] When elephants are left alive, their tusks can grow 7 inches a year and never stop growing. One bull had a 10-foot, 200-pound tusk!

[11] Researchers have found that elephants experience joy, grief, rage, compassion, stress, and love.

[12] 1 pound = $1,000.

into cash to support the black market. But there's no bringing those elephants back to life. It doesn't matter how many ships we intercept or how many smugglers we put behind bars. If the killers are still out there . . .

Sure, we've got wildlife patrols, but they can only cover so much ground. Where exactly on the vast continents of Africa and Asia are those animals being hunted? If only there were a way to track that ivory back to its source. To know just where—amongst the gajillion acres, preserves, and countries—those great gray beasts are being crumpled.

You know what we need? Dung, of course.

As dung goes slip-sliding through a gut, it gets coated with mucus and epithelial cells. Everyone's seen epithelial tissue on the outside of the body—we call it skin. The gut is lined with it, too. With every dump of dung, some of those epithelial cells hitchhike on the poop and escape the deep, dark tunnel of the digestive tract.[13] And inside each of those cells is that magical molecule we call DNA.

DNA is as powerful as a fingerprint. From the epithelial cells in a single dung sample, scientists can read the genetic code of a single elephant. But it gets better than that. Because related animals have similar DNA, if you collect samples from a bunch of elephants, you can make a map of elephant families across the land. Then, the next time law enforcement officers confiscate some ivory, they can slice off a sliver and dive into its DNA. Match up that code with ones on the map that are related . . . bull's-eye!

In 2015, when officials confiscated 50 large shipments of

---

[13] In the poop of a sea creature called a phyllosoma, a scientist found a thin film of epithelial cells wrapped tightly around the stinging cells of a jellyfish. So that's how a phyllosoma eats jellies without paying a painful price!

ivory,[14] they put this system to work. The DNA pointed to two poaching hotspots. The wildlife rangers circled the spots, nabbed the poachers, and shut down the largest elephant poaching cartels in all of Africa.

Think of all those trunks tooting in triumph! *This* is what poop can do.

Saving elephants is awesome, but what about animals who don't leave softball-sized turds? What about animals that are endangered *and* elusive? How can we find their poo? The Conservation Canines, a group out of the University of Washington, solved that problem by putting pups to work. The group turns unwanted dogs into lifesavers by training them to find the feces of bears, badgers, birds, bats, and even butterflies.

Now, Piper can sniff out some poo, but she's as likely to roll in it as politely alert me to its location. How do they train a dog to do that?

1) They visit an animal shelter and find the most hyper pup. The one the owners gave up on because she has too much energy—the border collie or cattle dog or good old-fashioned mutt who will chase a ball till she drops, then jump up and go again.

2) Then they spend a few months teaching the dog that if she'll sniff out the poop of one specific species and then sit down beside it, she'll get to play ball.

---

[14] Some shipments had 4,000 tusks!

3) Finally, they haul her into the field and collect some elusive poop!

Pangolins are one of the most highly poached mammals on the planet. Those scaly anteaters are also one of the most elusive. One researcher, Hyeon Jeong Kim, who goes by HJ, has been studying pangolins for 5 years. She has yet to see one in the wild. No one ever seems to find them, except, of course, the pangolin poachers.[15]

"There are 10-ton seizures, thousands of animals," HJ tells me on a video chat. That's a lot of pangolins captured, considering that pangolins aren't megamammals.

How big are they?

"Some of them are . . . an armful." HJ stretches her arms out in a circle. I imagine her hugging one of those bronze beauties.[16]

If you ever did see a pangolin, you'd love the way it can curl up, protected by scales. Scales like rows of gilded beech leaves in the fall. The scaly scales are so treasured that, once, someone stitched a bunch together to make a coat of armor for the Prince of Wales.[17]

---

[15] How do poachers find pangolins? Who knows! And there's no way poachers are spilling that secret.

[16] The largest pango ever recorded was a giant ground pangolin, weighing in at 72.6 pounds. On the other end of the scale is the long-tailed pangolin, at 4 to 6 pounds. That's like a boxer versus a Chihuahua.

[17] Pangolin scales are made of keratin—the same stuff in your fingernails and toenails.

HJ treasures the scales, too, but she'd rather see them on the animal. She's in a race against pangolin poaching. The anteaters are killed for their scales and their meat.[18] One day, HJ had a thought: poop maps save elephants, so why not pangolins? Should be easy, right?

Think again.

At the University of Washington, HJ was all keyed up to pull DNA from pangolin poo, but there's a problem. Remember that bit about it being hard to find pangolins? No pangolins, no poo. How do you train a dog with no droppings? Could she copycat Daniella and get some from the zoo? No dice. At that time, there were no pangolins in US zoos. Ask for a loan from Vietnam, China, or Thailand, where these ant-slurpers stroll around? Nope, that paperwork would have taken forever. There are laws protecting these animals, laws that make it illegal to ship the animals (or their parts) across borders. So, two dogs (Athena and Skye)[19] and two handlers (Jennifer Hartman and Suzie Marlow) flew into Nepal without even knowing what pango poo smells (or looks) like.

I had a video chat with Jennifer, too. She told me that she went in thinking, "This is what we do best. I've got this." But things weren't all that easy.

For one thing, there were the leeches. When Skye went for a swim, little leeches swam up the dog's nose. Later, big leeches had to be dragged back out. Jennifer wiggled a finger in front of her

---

[18] There are 8 different species of pangolins. How many of each? They are so shy no one's been able to count them.

[19] Skye is an Australian kelpie mix who's a pro at finding fisher and marten poo. Athena's a black-and-white-and-tan Australian shepherd who is also trained to find bird and bat carcasses on a wind farm.

face, showing me what it looked like. Poor Skye was sneezing blood for days.

The second thing that wasn't so easy? Finding poop for training the dogs. In the Rani Community Forest, they got some translators, they got permission from the village elders, and they got some local help. They searched and searched, but for all that effort, all they could identify were rat droppings, leaf matter, and porcupine poo. Then they realized, *no one* knew what pangolin poo looked like. Day after day, the dogs were bored in their kennels, waiting for a whiff to learn the odor of precious pango poo.

One day, a village elder in flip-flops led Jennifer and Suzie on a trek deep into the forest. They whacked their way through the vegetation and clambered up steep slopes. A pangolin burrow! That burrow, though, was filled with dead leaves. It hadn't been used in years. Then, Jennifer got a sneaky suspicion. Who would know, in all this forest, where pangolins had been hiding out? Poachers. What if the people leading her were actually poachers?![20] What if they were just taking her on a wild goose chase?

The stress had built up, the dogs were antsy, the team had lost a week of precious time, when finally, finally there was a pile. It wasn't the poop of any animal they knew—not monkey, not porcupine, not rat.

Was it really pangolin poo? It just *had* to be.

So, they trusted it was and trained the dogs.

"Sit. Ball. Data." That's the way it is supposed to go. The dog is

---

[20]It's easy for me to point a finger at poachers. *I* never eat pangolins or buy their scales. But pangolins also lose out when their habitat is mined for bauxite. Bauxite is aluminum. Aluminum in the can in my hand and the phone in my pocket. The average American consumes ~5,677 pounds of bauxite over a lifetime.

trained to find the poop and sit beside it to alert the handler. Then the dog gets to play ball, and the handler collects the data (date, location, etc.).

One day after the fieldwork had begun, Athena did something odd. Instead of sitting or continuing to sniff, she brushed at dead leaves with her paw.

Jennifer peered down. No poop.

Why was Athena breaking the rules? Maybe, Jennifer figured, it was because Athena was being asked to perform after only a short training; maybe she was still learning the smell of those Nepalese leaves. But it didn't quite make sense.

Jennifer stooped down and looked under the leaves. No poop. Then she dug a bit.

Sparkly dirt. As Jennifer was telling me this, the bat guano sparkling under the microscope popped back into my mind. Hey, pangolins eat bugs, too!

That day, Athena taught Jennifer—and the world—that Chinese pangolins bury their business.[21]

Another day, Suzie and Skye were out in the forest with a ranger. Skye alerted at a tree. There was a hole in the tree, so of course the people took a look. While she recounted this tale about Suzie, Jennifer's hands rose up and her index fingers pointed down. "Pangolin," she whispered. Even the forest ranger had never seen one in the wild before. They were so excited, they just started hugging—two strangers out in the middle of the jungle, hugging for joy at one little curled cutie.

I wanted to know: what does pangolin poop smell like?

---

[21] But apparently other pangolin species don't. I wonder why.

Jennifer said, "I love poop. I collect poop for a living. Wolf scat is stinky. Marten and fisher and mink actually have a sweet musk odor. They are lovely and I would wear it as a perfume. Pangolin? One of the most foul."

Why? All they eat are insects. My bat guano wasn't rank. Maybe pangolins eat other things, too? No one knows . . . yet.

After a month and a half of sweaty work in the field, Athena and Skye had sniffed out 35 samples. Fortunately, Jennifer and Suzie didn't have to cart the super stinky poo home in their suitcases. They stashed it in a freezer in Nepal. Poop stays in the country where it is found.

While Jennifer and Suzie were bouncing around in the woods, HJ was nose-down in the lab, laying plans for those little treasures. Just like with the elephants, HJ will be extracting DNA from the pangolin epithelial cells. During that trip to Nepal, HJ had figured a few things out, but the real work on those samples will have to wait for her next trip.

On our video chat, HJ explained the steps she'll take when she gets back. She'll split open the cells and wash the DNA. Don't go thinking she's doing this in her kitchen sink. It's all microscopic and each step has its own laboratory technique. DNA sticks to a filter so she can wash the other, um, "stuff" on through. Then, hopefully, she'll get this blob of DNA in a tube. But what if the sample didn't arrive quickly enough and has grown white mold? What if the DNA is too broken into bits and pieces? What if she makes a mistake?

I watched worry wash across HJ's face.

Only 35 fresh samples. It could all swish down the drain.

Unlike with other species where scientists have already figured things out, HJ is *the* scientist developing the procedures for how all this is done. Some days she tries out a technique and has to wait 3 days to know if it works or not. There's no worksheet giving her the instructions. No one's ever played this game with pangolin poo before.

"It's so scary," she admitted, "because we don't know how many [pangolins] are out there, so we don't know how many we've lost or what percentage is left or . . ."

HJ can't just curl up into a ball and hide from those hurdles. I could feel her fear, but sitting here today, thinking back on how far they have come, a different emotion begins to take over.

Daniella and Jennifer and Suzie and HJ and I, we have this dream. It's a dream of a world that looks different. A world where people let great gray beasts and little bronze beauties keep doing their thing.

No, we can't wave our hands over a black hat, shout "Abraca-dabra!" and pull out a map to find the poachers. Yes, there are still hurdles to leap. But a zing of hope is zipping through my heart and my hands. Those beasts and beauties have a team of animal lovers, a slew of smart scientists, and a pack of poo-sniffing pooches on their side.

I just know HJ will figure this out.

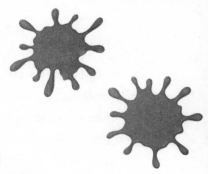

CHAPTER 5

STOOL TO FUEL

Imagine a tinkerer, someone squirreled away in a workshop underground. Or an inventor who works into the wee hours of the morning, creating contraptions. Or maybe a mad scientist with a brain that whizzes and whirls, gushes and rushes, cranks and creates so many ideas that they keep spilling right out.

Now imagine all those people wrapped up in one. That is Brian Harper.

He's the guy who helped introduce the idea of thermal imaging—the stuff firefighters now use to see through smoke and save thousands of lives. The guy who, when he worked for the queen of England, had 8 soldiers guarding his top-secret efforts. The guy whose camera system kept the space shuttle safe.[1]

But none of *that* made Brian Harper famous. No, to get 7 million hits on the internet, he needed a streetlamp and some doggie doo-doo. Brian Harper wanted to turn dog stool into fuel. Not a kitchen stool or a piano stool—the kind of stool that comes from rear ends!

---

[1] When hydrogen burns you don't see flame, just a shimmer. On the space shuttle launchpad in the heat of Florida, everything shimmers. How to spot a stray fire during countdown? You need a special camera.

Brilliant! I wanted to try that. So, I scooped up some Piper poo, but—P U—decided cow patties would work just as well.[2] Better, perhaps. Think of all the chopped-up grass in there.

Why, yes, those *are* cow pies drying on my front porch.

I don't have a streetlamp to light, but I have a cup of tea to brew. So, one November morning, I squat in my driveway, break open a crispy cow patty, and pull out my new lighter with its long, flexible wand. It's 26°F and my eyes are smarting in the wind. No problem. I'll have this fire roaring in a jiffy.[3]

Holding a patty, I pluck away the pebbles and think about what I'm actually holding. Solidified sunlight.

Some grass plant grabbed carbon dioxide out of thin air, water from the soil, and energy that traveled 92,955,807 miles from the sun. And with just those ingredients, it made sugar.

Photosynthesis

$$6CO_2 + 6H_2O + Sunlight \rightarrow C_6H_{12}O_6 + 6O_2[4]$$

A blade of grass did that! A blade of grass that I step on without even thinking about it. Photosynthesis astounds me and surrounds me. On top of that, the grass zip-zapped a bunch of those sugar molecules together with chemical bonds. The result is a super long, super strong, super waterproof molecule—

Cellulose.

---

[2] Did you know you can buy cow pies over the internet? I got mine from a neighbor, but who knew?!

[3] The driveway gravel won't burn, but I have water on hand in case Mr. Fire rages out of hand.

[4] CO_2: carbon dioxide; H_2O: water; $C_6H_{12}O_6$: sugar; O_2: oxygen.

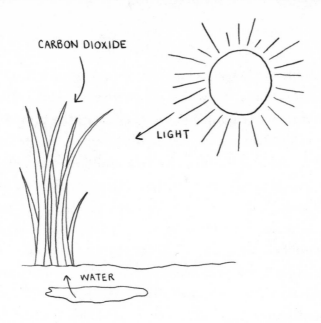

CARBON DIOXIDE

LIGHT

WATER

It's the most common organic[5] compound on Earth. It is in the wall of every plant cell on the planet, holds up giant redwood trees, and is the basis of just about every item I prize. My house? Made of cellulose (we call it wood). My books? Made of cellulose (paper). My food? Made with cellulose (apples, salsa, milkshakes)![6]

And now, I'm about to use the magic of combustion to undo photosynthesis and snap all those energy-packed chemical bonds. The fire will release a whole slew of energy back into the air.

Flick, flick. My fancy new lighter flashes. Orange warms the fringes of the pie, but then it goes gray instead of catching. Hmm. Maybe it needs more oxygen. *Crunch-crunch.* I mash the pie till it looks like crumbled shredded wheat cereal.

Flick, flick. Nothing. I slip inside for matches instead. The

---

[5] "Organic" as in it contains carbon and was once alive, not as in "organically grown apples"—although organically grown apples are full of organic compounds. ☺

[6] Restaurants add cellulose to milkshakes to make them thick and creamy! And, of course, the cows ate cellulose.

warmth of the kitchen envelops me. My stove volunteers: I'm here! My tea kettle stands ready. No. The stove uses electricity. I've seen entire forests hacked down to dig coal out of the ground, streams turned orange, smokestacks belching toxins. All to make that electricity. Today, I'll leave that 300-million-year-old solidified sunlight[7] right in the ground where it belongs. To brew my tea, I'm using biofuel.

Half a book of matches later, my pyro pride is evaporating. A lifetime of campfires and I can't get this poop to light! People all over the world have been burning herbivore dung (cow in India, llama in South America, bison in North America) to heat their homes and stoves. How do they do it? I duck inside again and return with a pile of newspaper and my secret ingredient: drier lint.

I wad up the paper, ball up the lint, and lean flakes of the dung up against one another to allow space for the oxygen to flow in. Perched on a metal cooking grate above my fire-to-be, my cup waits patiently.

Fffft. Sssss. The newspaper catches. Wind whips the flame. FIRE! The smoke is musty, all sage and smudge. One flaky fringe of the cow pie glows. An orange wave creeps across its surface like moving magma. I stretch my fingers to the meager heat.

A whisp, a curtain, a curl of smoke rises. "Oh, thank you," I whisper, setting a tea bag into the cup. But the cow pie is turning black. Why won't it burn?

Sigh. Nothing's ever easy.

Without even needing tongs, I reach in and crush a crumble

---

[7] Ancient ferns the size of trees fell down in the muck, got covered up, and after millions of years were packed solid into a thing we call coal.

into shreds. There's a small glow. I lean in and blow, feeding oxygen to the heart of the heat. Blow and blow and blow till I'm dizzy. I dip my pinkie into the cup. Cold.

Grr. The cooking rack clatters as I knock it aside. I settle the cup directly on the coals. In the cup, chestnut-brown color leaks from the tea bag and fingers its way into the water. Gray swirlies float up from the fire and land in my water. Maybe only the newspaper is light enough to do that?

When the water is solid brown, I lift the cup, curl my hand around, and sip. Not hot. There is tea flavor, but also something cottony and tasting of chemicals. Not the hay-scented tea I had hoped for. Not something I can swallow.

An hour, an entire newspaper, and far too many matches later, I retreat to my fossil-fueled home, my pyro pride tucked between my legs.

How did he do it, that Brian Harper and his doggie stool?

Later, Brian told me the whole thing started because of some antique streetlamps in his hometown, Malvern Hills, England, a land of castles, cathedrals, historic hills, and holy spring water. In that kind of setting, modern streetlights just wouldn't do. But with all the expenses of gas and maintenance, those picturesque lamps were going to be cut off. What would those lamps do, standing around bored every night?[8]

When we spoke, Brian was sitting in front of shelves so heavy

---

[8] The authors C. S. Lewis and J. R. R. Tolkien used to meet in Malvern, and some say one of those lamps inspired Lewis's *The Lion, The Witch and The Wardrobe.*

with books and notebooks I was sure they would all topple right over on top of him. Notes and scribbled scraps of paper threatened to leap off the bulletin board at his right. I smiled when he talked; he's all "bloody" this and that, tossing trash into "bins," and studying in "la-BOR-a-tories." Gotta love those Brits!

A group of environmentally minded townspeople—they called themselves "the Gasketeers," like the Three Musketeers—banded together. They wanted to run the lamps on biogas. Biogas is a fuel you get by putting mighty microbes to work on organic matter and letting them basically fart out useful gas. Then, you burn that gas, which is mostly methane (or, if you are Brian, "MEE-thane"), the flammable stuff also found in cow burps.

Oh. Brian wasn't just *burning* poo like I'd tried to do. His ideas were a tad more sophisticated, and the idea of using biogas really revved him up. "If you could, it would be zero carbon,[9] because it is renewable fuel, not fossil fuels." I'll take renewable over fossil fuels any day. Renewable fuels, like solar or waterpower, can be replaced within a person's lifetime. Fossil fuels, like coal or oil, take millions of years to replace.

Where in this quaint little town could you get enough organic matter to generate biogas?

Puppy poo to the rescue!

Around Brian Harper's house, puppy poo is a problem. He's on the main path, just 100 yards from a ridgeline where everyone, *everyone* goes to walk their dog. "A lot gets left in plastic bags in the trees, swinging around for years. In the winter it is like you put Christmas decorations in the trees, but it's black. Horrible."

---

[9] Carbon released – carbon taken in = zero carbon.

Brian decided to build a special gas lantern that used a biodigester system—a contraption for converting stool into fuel. First, though, he needed to know more about doggie doo.

It's a good thing Brian Harper has a tough stomach. For three weeks he dug through the doggie doo bins to see what he would find. "You have crisp packets, sweets wrappers,[10] a dead falcon." And then there's a whole variety of dog poo. "A terrier produces almost nothing, 100 grams, 200 grams if you are lucky. An average dog poo is about three-quarters of a pound, by the way. Get yourself up to a Labrador or a Great Dane—it's the size of human poo."

Hunkered in his lab, Brian dug into the scientific papers, hoping for some help. He found two groups who had succeeded in turning feces into fuel in dog parks, an artist in Massachusetts and a group of students in Arizona. Both were cool projects. Both worked . . . for a little while.

But, nothing's ever easy.

"You've got to have it 30° centigrade for the microbes to do their work." Arizona was too hot in the summer; Massachusetts too cold in the winter. On top of that, Brian couldn't find anything written down about their biodigester designs. He found a lady in Canada who knew tons about biodigesters but nothing about using dog poo.

After 2 years of research, Brian started tinkering. "Then there's loads of experimental work on how much gas we could make from what weight of dog poo and also how a biodigester reacts to only being fed dog poo."

Creating the contraption required massive amounts of engineering, and then he had to teach people to use it—correctly. One

---

[10] Translation: crisps = french fries; sweets = candy.

little innocent plastic bag—used instead of the perfectly good, perfectly free paper bag Brian provided—can gum up the works. And who do you think has to rake through the muck to fish it out?

Finally, Brian had a prototype: a big green bin, with a hatch and a crank, sitting at the base of the lamp. During the day, dog walkers toss the doo-doo down the hatch, crank it 5 times (to stir it all up), and head off on their merry way. Down in that hopper, magic happens. Not really—it's biology and chemistry and physics. You can think of the microbes as munching, but we science nerds call it fermentation. Their food is that organic matter, and their waste is 60 percent methane and 40 percent carbon dioxide,[11] with a smidge of hydrogen sulfide.[12] The gas gets stored in a tank. The other leftovers, called digestate, drip out a pipe and can be used as fertilizer.

At night, a sensor flips the switch, releasing the methane from the tank, and *flick*! The lamp is lit!

Today, dogs and their walkers pass Brian's lamp on purpose. One gal drives in from miles away to walk 6 dogs. No sense toting all those stinky bags home.

Did I mention that Brian's story went viral? People come from all over the world—a TV station in Japan, a guide dog training center, a park in Pennsylvania—to discover how to use up doo-doo, too.

Brian's not done tinkering yet. What's next? Making the K9 Bio Digester look like a dog. Open up the

---

[11] $CH_3COOH => CH_4 + CO_2$
[12] That's the rotten-egg smell. P U.

mouth; drop in the poop. Let the digestate dribble out the tail end. Plant pretty flowers in that. And what about a barbecue? Hot dogs cooked by doggie doo![13]

Almost 3 hours later when our conversation is over, my cheeks hurt from grinning so much. Think of what Brian's brainpower earned him:

1) a street without doggie doo. In the UK, about 700,000 pounds of puppy poo are produced per year.[14]
2) a landfill *not* filled with poopy bags. In a landfill, microbes convert poo into methane. If released into the atmosphere, methane is 20 to 30 times more potent in trapping heat than carbon dioxide.
3) a fossil fuel–free flicker to light his street. Just 10 bags of doo-doo provide an hour of light. Homegrown green power!

---

[13] Brian's even got plans to pipe the leftover carbon dioxide into a greenhouse to grow bigger, better tomatoes. Or maybe compress it into a cylinder to use in fizzy drinks. Don't you want a swig?

[14] In America, it may be closer to 10 million tons per year.

CHAPTER 6
GOT GUTS?

A long line of gut stretched across my deck. It was pink, looked like a flattened garden hose, and held nut-sized fecal lumps. The antiseptic odor reminded me of a doctor's office. I stood there, hands on my hips, and asked Piper, "Why would an animal need 18 feet of small intestine?"

And how had it all fit into a beaver body that was only 27 inches long? Sure, I was the one who had just extricated it from the belly, but it was like one of those magic tricks where the colored handkerchiefs just keep coming and coming out of the hat.

I should clarify, I never meant to go cutting into dead bodies, that's not where this started, but once I was elbow-deep, yanking on a string of intestines, I couldn't stop. And it wasn't just one beaver. There was a bunny, a fawn, a bobcat, a river otter, and a kingsnake.[1]

It had started at 9:10 on Friday night when my friend texted me a screenshot. Clicking through, I discovered this project called "Got Guts?" They were begging people to send in pics of an animal's

---

[1] If you are wondering where I got all those dead bodies, every one of those sweethearts' sweet hearts stopped pumping on the road. ☻

gut including the cecum. Awesome! I had a camera; I could get my hands on some guts. I didn't really understand what a cecum was, but I was going to contribute to science!

Staring down at the mangled beaver body, I realized I should have read the instructions first. It was kind of too late for "Step 2: Take a picture of the whole body, with a coin or other scale object of known length." And when I actually went step-by-step and registered on the website like I was supposed to, I saw they weren't even interested in beaver ceca.[2] Hey, who are these people and how come they're discriminating against bodacious bucktoothed beavers?

Then, I reread the instructions. "Step 1: Go hunting or fishing as usual."

Duh, Heather. Beaver aren't your "usual" game species here in Alabama. Why were these scientists so interested in deer or fish or rabbit ceca? The About page was a total tease: mammals have a cecum (usually). Birds have two. And fish, theirs are in the "wrong" place, up between the stomach and intestine instead of between the small and large intestine where they belong.

At the bottom of the page was that tantalizing little line: "Learn more."

Click!

I spent the rest of my Sunday leaping from link to link and plowing through scientific papers I found on the site. Each paper had me swimming through words I didn't quite understand, yet managed to utterly fascinate me.[3] I tracked down one of the project

---

[2] *Ceca*: plural of *cecum*. Gee, isn't spelling fun?
[3] An example of those papers: "Let them eat leaves: The critical role of dietary foliage in maintaining the gut microbiome and metabolome of folivorous sifakas."

leaders, Dr. Erin McKenney at North Carolina State University, to ask for some answers.

Erin loves lemurs, those long-tailed, pop-eyed primates that live only on the island of Madagascar. Once upon a time, lemur ancestors lived on the continent that is now called Africa. About 55 million years ago, another group of primates, the monkeys and apes, evolved. They were big and better at getting the grub than lemurs were. All across the mainland, lemurs went extinct. One, two, three, who knows how many lemur species winked out. But lemurs still lurked high in the trees on Madagascar. No other primates made it to that island.[4] With all those treetop treats to themselves, lemurs flourished. They evolved to take advantage of that cornucopia of food. Some evolved to eat fruits, some dined exclusively on leaves, others chomped it all down.

What part of lemurs fascinates Erin? The guts, of course.

A gut is a glorious thing.

Erin started our video chat by describing the gut as a river of nutrients. This lady speaks my language!

"The difference," she said, "is, the riverbank of your gut is also absorbing things out of the stream." The nutrients change as they move through that river. As she talked, my mind flashed to guts I had explored and notes from my journals.

"Your saliva starts to break down the starch in your mouth."

12/3/18   Deer Fawn Gut   Shed   56° & Partially Overcast

In the roof of the fawn's mouth—rows of indentations that look like black roof tiles. What are they for? Run my

---

[4] How did the lemurs get there? No one knows. Some hypothesize that they were there all along, but others think they hitched a ride on trees floating across from the mainland.

tongue in the top of my mouth—I have a few, too. Inside her cheeks, something like hairs. Light gray and tooth-shaped. What do those do? Odor is fetid. Snip my way along esophagus—down, down, down into glip and glop. Odor turns sour. The stomach is like crumpled grocery store bags.[5]

"Your stomach is where the protein gets digested."

10/6/17   Bobcat Dissection   Side yard   Upper 80s & Sticky
Stomach = white-pink pouch like a stuffed fanny pack. Thin lines stretch across the sheet of muscle. Scalpel slices; gas hisses; pouch deflates. Wet hair (short, dark) outlines the shape of a body.[6] Oh. A gray nose fringed with a fuzz of brown hair. A skull fragment, spiky and jagged, ready to stab through my gloves. A clear lump that must be the lens of an eye. A tail the right length for a chipmunk.

"The small intestine is where your fats get digested, right?"

12/17/18   River Otter Intestines   Dining Room   Sunny & 55°
A jelly-like mass oozes out of a bulge in the intestine. It's the pink of the heavens at sunset. Digested flesh? It sticks to my gloves like wet lips. Mucus? Between my

---

[5] Deer stomachs change with the season. It makes sense—a spring salad of young grass is quite different from a fall feast of acorns.

[6] Do bobcats hack up hairballs from their prey? My cat Annie's a pro at hacking up hair from her grooming. Apparently some goes through her gut, too. One day I cut through her turd and found a wad tucked in the center. A Tootsie Roll treat!

fingers—squish. Something gritty in the center. Fish parts? The smell of fish, but under loupe, bits of shell remind me of frozen waves, sculpted crinkles, armor finer than that of a samurai. There's frozen foam and hairs like spines. A serrated blade. A forest of prickers. Then, off by itself sits an exquisite arch. A crayfish antenna!

Why have I never marveled at the intricacies of a crayfish before?

"The colon is your last chance to suck out all the nutrients and the water before you poop."

12/19/18   **Kingsnake Gut**   **Dining Room Table**   40s & Cloudy
Prospecting up from rectum (dark and lumpy). Something the size of a rice grain sticks to the outside. Colon diameter = two coffee stirrers. Stretchy—equally stretchy on all sides. Moving up the tube, a wad of brown mush. Snip of grass blade—from prey stomach? Amber-brown bead shaped like a spaceship. Seed? An ant with his head cocked sideways. Sand. Gray-pink jelly. A tooth! A single pointed tooth. The tip is angled; the other end teardrop shape. This snake's? From prey? From another snake?

"And those are all things," Erin says, "the body is doing by itself with no help. So, by the time your food gets to the colon, you've taken out the starch while it's in your mouth, you've taken out the protein in the stomach, you've taken out the fat in your small intestine, so all that's left is fiber—"

Remember cellulose? That tough stuff in plant cells? That's fiber.

"—which no animal on the planet can digest by itself. So how," she pauses, "are there herbivores?"

Those giraffes, those elephants, that beaver, that bunny . . .

"They shouldn't exist. The only reason there are any animals on the entire planet that eat plants is because of gut microbes." An intestine is packed with teeny, tiny, microscopic organisms who think fiber is fantastic. When Erin talks about her favorite herbivores, lemurs, she calls them a "bag of bugs."

"If you are a carnivore, you can afford to have a short, fast gut, because you can digest the protein and fat by yourself. So, you have a really short gut—3 to 4 times the length of your body. Herbivores, on the other hand, are going to have s-u-u-u-per long colons and/or that really big stomach if you are a cow or a deer or a sheep."[7]

When a deer (or any other ruminant) eats, it scarfs down the grass and stashes it in its "first" stomach. Microbes begin to break it down. Then the deer coughs up its cud to chew a second time.[8] That gives the deer guts a second chance to chomp up the cellulose in those plant cells and a first chance to mash up those microbes. Those microbes are the only thing keeping a deer alive.

"And there's another way, too," Erin continues. "Sometimes you have a cecum."

Microbes need time and space to work. When you eat lots of cellulose, the microbes need that river to slow down.

---

[7] Those big stomachs have 4 parts: (1) the rumen, a big sack with lots of room to hold food and microbes, (2) the reticulum, where microbes live and ferment chewed food, (3) the omasum, which absorbs liquid and makes sure no big pieces get through, and (4) the abomasum, where acid is added and digestion occurs.

[8] I wanna know, does it taste like vomit? Erin filled me in: Part of our vomit's flavor and burn is due to stomach acid. Deer cud wouldn't be acidic because that would kill all their microbes. She's never tasted it but thinks it would taste like fresh grass.

"Your food will be going down, down, down through the small intestines and then it just kind of gets lost in this huge pocket between the small intestine and the large intestine."

A pocket called a cecum.

1/27/19   Beaver Gut   Front Porch   Sunny & Upper 40s

The beaver cecum is a massive pink bag the shape of a seahorse. At least 11 inches long. Unlike the tan, chiseled wood chips and bright green leafy bits in the stomach, the stuff in the cecum is a pea-green soup.[9] At the head of it, wood fibers grit between my fingers. As I make my way out to the tail end, it gets more pasty and yellow till it is pudding smooth. When I zoom in with the scope, the contents go from being green gunk to an exquisite froth. Bubbles peer up at me like the eyes of an owl.

"Suffice it to say, a cecum is a great place for the river of nutrients to just kind of eddy and wander around."

Whether you are a beaver or a bunny, the cecum is just the place for microbes to process all that paste and turn it into pellets.

Cool!

So, what does all this have to do with "Got Guts?"

"The thing is, the cecum is the only site in your gut that is there for microbes and not for you. A lot of different animals have evolved a cecum, and that's because the cecum gives you a haven for beneficial microbes. If you ever have a flooding of the river,

---

[9] Some people say beaver eat fish. But investigate their intestines and it's obvious they are all herbivore. One of their favorite dishes: the inner bark of an aspen tree. That's where a tissue called phloem lets sugar flow from the leaves down to the rest of the tree.

that washes away your native microbes. Then everything else is washed away except for in that eddy pool." That little pocket harboring microbes can reseed the gut.

The crazy thing is, we know very little about animal ceca. Even Erin has trouble getting diagrams of certain species' guts. We don't know how different one species is from the next. On top of that, as the Got Guts? website says, "we have no idea how much one individual varies from another."

The only way to really discover all this variation is to examine lots and lots and lots of guts. If you wanted to know if the size of a person's hand affects their ability to throw a football, you'd measure a bunch of hands and compare that to how far those people can throw. But how often do you get a chance to peek into a gut, not to mention actually measure it?

So, you can see Erin's problem. There are so many species out there, they vary so much, and most folks don't have guts just lying around. But there's a group of folks who do...

If you hunt or fish, and if you gut what you catch, you've got the guts Erin needs.

Hunters send Erin pics. From that, she'll learn just one basic thing—how big the ceca are. But that basic information is more than we currently know. How are we supposed to help animals if we don't even know these basics? Hunters will help.

By looking at the digestive tracts of captive lemurs, Erin knows just how much they can vary from species to species.[10] The sifaka eat only leaves. Leaves = fiber. Their guts are about 16 times the

---

[10] Never waste a dead body. ☺ Even when a lemur dies of disease or other natural causes, he has lots to teach us.

length of their bodies. Red ruffed lemurs eat only fruit. Fruit = sugar. Put a red ruffed gut up against that of a sifaka, and it looks puny! Ring-tailed lemurs eat fruit and veggies. Veggies = fiber. Their gut length lines up right in the middle of the red ruffed and the sifaka. There are 113 different species of lemurs. Think of the variety hiding out in their tummies!

Lemurs are one of the most threatened groups of mammals on the planet. If you are one of the special people at the Duke Lemur Center entrusted with keeping lemurs alive in captivity, do you care about their ceca? Um, yes.

Erin's earlier research is already helping lemurs. Her "Got Guts?" project will help bears and deer and fish, but there's another species she's curious about.

"So, I measured a lot of humans last fall," she says with a deadpan face.

I laugh. Can you imagine her running around a mall with a tape measure? But then I realize she's not talking about living humans. "Are you serious?"

"I'm working on the paper this afternoon." Even within our species, she explains, there is so much we don't know. "Nobody's really studied the variation in the human gut since 1850."

No way!

"Until a colleague and I went to measure cadavers in Duke's anatomy lab last fall."[11]

---

[11] Studying the guts of cadavers might be better than studying live ones. In the 1820s, when a man's stomach gunshot wound wouldn't heal shut, Dr. William Beaumont kept it open so he could experiment. Experiments that included licking the man's stomach lining to see if it was acidic!

WOW.

Now Erin and her team of students are busy analyzing that data. "It's a cool story."

What might that data reveal? What does my cecum look like? My brother is a vegan. Is his gut different from mine?

Erin's study isn't finished yet. She can't fill me in on that cool story yet, but just think of what she might discover![12]

---

[12] One thing she could tell me: women's small intestines are larger and longer than men's. Just one more mystery looking for answers!

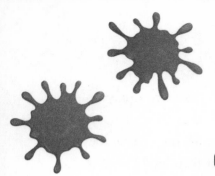

CHAPTER 7

SURVIVAL

It was warm and squishy in my palm. The aroma wafted out of the plastic bag and up to my nose. That nippy, misty morning, instead of letting the bag of Piper's doggie doo dangle from my fingertips, I cradled the crap in my hand. Then, I shoved up my sweater and pressed it to my belly.

You *might* be able to use fresh poop as a hand warmer, but as the bag crinkled against my skin, I wasn't convinced it could save my life. Bear Grylls, that survival guy on television, claimed it could. Sure, on extreme TV he might drink water wrung from elephant dung,[1] but in the real world, could poop save a life? That's the question that, months later, had me trekking across New York City's Central Park and striding into Mount Sinai Hospital.

Meet Dr. Ari Grinspan. With his official title, his spick-and-span office, and his pinstriped shirt, I could have assumed Dr. Grinspan was a straitlaced kind of guy. But a few things told me otherwise:

---

[1] I've never been at risk of dying from dehydration, so I haven't tried it myself, but I suppose a swallow of mysterious microbes would have to be better than death.

1) The prize possession in his office: coffee beans from the poop of an Asian palm civet.[2]
2) A favorite memory from his childhood: poop jokes with his dad and three brothers.
3) His career: peering inside human rear ends!

I had come to Ari's office to get a tour of a living, breathing[3] human colon. Ari is a gastroenterologist. One of the tools of his trade: a camera he sticks up people's backside to see what's going on in there. Another cool tool: stool.

Ari leaned across his desk and told me, "The stuff you are flushing is incredibly complex. It's rich, it's diverse, and it plays a huge role in who we are."

Do you remember those fiber-chomping microbes in animal guts? That's what Ari's talking about, but he's not talking about a species here and a species there; he's talking about an entire biome, the microbiome, swirling inside your body. It's as complex as a rainforest—viruses, fungi, protozoans, and our favorite little guys: bacteria! That complexity (called biodiversity) is the key to a healthy microbiome. In addition to helping digest your food, those little Pac-men make vitamins your body needs[4] and play ninja against the bad guys. Sure, some microbes are parasites, but most help you out. You take care of them; they take care of you. A win-win!

---

[2] World's most expensive coffee! Usually, people pick the cherrylike fruit of the coffee tree, then ferment, roast, and grind the seeds. But civets eat the coffee fruit, seed and all, so why not let them do all that picking and fermentation work?

[3] Scratch that—people don't breathe through their rear ends, but the endangered Mary River turtle can. It sucks in water, extracts the oxygen, and hangs out underwater for up to 72 hours! A great way to avoid predators—not so great for avoiding water pollution. ☹

[4] Vitamin K, for example, is made *in* your body but not *by* your body. Without vitamin K, your blood won't clot, and you could bleed to death from a single cut. Thanks, bacteria!

Trillions of microbial cells (about 3 pounds)[5] live in and on a human. That's 10 times as many microbes as human cells in the body. Crazy. Imagine an entire biome—something as awesome as a rainforest—all worming, squirming, and earning their keep inside your intestines.

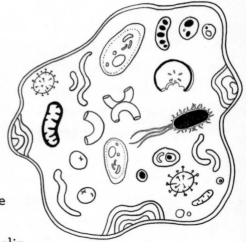

And some of those guys come slip-sliding out into the toilet. Peer down in the pot and you think it is all leftover food—wrong!

75% water

The solid part:

30% bacteria (dead and alive)
30% fiber from food
40% inorganic stuff plus dead blood cells, etc.[6]

Next time you go counting, you will find about 100 billion bacterial cells in one gram[7] of healthy human stool.

Where do we get our bacteria from in the first place?

"On this table, on my skin, in my mouth," Ari says. *"Everywhere."* For a baby, it starts the day she is born. Microbes from

---

[5] That's about as heavy as your brain.

[6] Why is your poo brown? Orange bilirubin mixes with yellow bile to paint poo a beautiful brown! Unless you eat beets or electric blue icing, which can turn your poo red or bright blue.

[7] Officially, a gram is the weight of a cubic centimeter of water. Unofficially, it's the weight of a dollar bill.

the mother's birth canal go up the nose and into the mouth. Or if she's lifted out of her mother in a C-section, it starts with the first person to touch her. "A mother's skin feeds the newborn's microbiome. That might actually be important, but we don't yet know."

With every inhale, every swallow, she'll be picking up microbes for the rest of her life. Ari's kids, who are growing up on the 32nd floor in a city, will cultivate a different community of microbes than kids who live in the outback of Australia.

"It's not like there are the 'right' bugs that should be in your colon. Everyone's different," he tells me. "The bugs in my intestines are different than yours, they are different than my wife's, but I'm sure there is a lot of similarity because we live in the same house, we eat the same food, and we share a lot of the same things, just like my two kids."

Think of it, every human on the planet has a unique microbiome. It's like a fingerprint.

"At age three is when we think it becomes finalized, becomes the adult biome, and you keep a lot of those bugs the rest of your life."

"Just because they settle in there so well?" I ask.

Ari's wicked grin comes out. "Unclear. We don't know." He loves unsolved mysteries of science, and the microbiome is one of the greatest unsolved mysteries of our time.

Next, Ari took me for a trip inside a colon.[8] He pulled up a video on his screen. It's like a roller coaster where we are being

---

[8] During a colonoscopy, you slide a tiny camera inside a patient's colon and take a look around. Think of it as a trip through innerspace.

pulled through a dark tunnel. The walls, the ceiling, the floor, are pink and pulsing. Just up ahead, it curves, making me eager to see what's around the corner.

"The reason why it is moving is because the patient's breathing in and out," he explained. "See the nice little blood vessels, it is pink. It's healthy. This is what the colon looks like." Well, a healthy colon.

Then Ari clicked on a new video and we plunged into a different world.

A throbbing hot red tunnel coated with globs of yellow gunk.

"All this yellow stuff is essentially the toxin from infection. It is toxic to the cells that make up the wall of the colon. Those cells explode like a volcano—"

You know the mustard-colored snot that comes out when you have a head cold? Imagine miniature mountains of that plastering your innards.

"—it is mucus, slimy, yellow—it's disgusting."

Meet *Clostridioides difficile*: a superbug nicknamed *C. diff*. He is not your friend. If you went to his family reunion, you'd meet his scummy cousins, which cause botulism, tetanus, and gas gangrene.[9] *C. diff*'s claim to fame? Diarrhea. Explosive diarrhea.

Stacked up against his cousins' handiwork, diarrhea might not seem like a big deal. Each year in America, half a million people have *C. diff* infections.

Each year, 29,000 of them die.

---

[9] What can those bad boys do? Botulism = paralysis of the face, limbs, lungs. Tetanus = toxin locks onto the ends of your nerves, your jaws clamp tight, you struggle to breathe. Gas gangrene = your skin bubbles and crackles as your muscles rot.

Months earlier, I had met a spunky gal who had faced off with *C. diff* several years before. Lauren Guintini's fight didn't start with *C. diff*; it started with a bacterial infection that landed her on the operating room table, where they said she might have to lose her leg.

The bacteria, a strain of staph[10] that took up residence under Lauren's skin, had super-morphing powers—it could slip right through the fingers of most antibiotic drugs.[11] One day when her leg was just about healed, Lauren went to the bathroom and out gushed blood and mucus—yellow mucus. Lauren had a case of *C. diff.*

To fight the staph, she had taken round after round of antibiotics. Antibiotics—the modern cure for everything that attacks us—get an A+ when it comes to killing off bacteria. The thing is, they had axed the good guys in Lauren's guts, too. Think of all the good guys that get axed when a rainforest gets hacked. In my neck of the woods, one of the first things to grow back after you cut the trees is poison ivy. Imagine a forest of that. In Lauren's gut, it was *C. diff.*

To fight that off, she had to gulp down more antibiotics. After a month or so, she'd get things under control and stop taking the antibiotics. Then *C. diff* would rear its nasty head and start exploding her gut cells again. And again. And again. Lauren was 16, taking 16 pills a day. She missed so much school they threatened to fail her. Her diarrhea was so bad she pooped her pants.

Lauren fought *C. diff* for years. Years of explosive diarrhea, a sharp stabbing in her gut, and slimy mucus pouring out. There

---

[10] If you want to get formal, call him Methicillin-resistant *Staphylococcus aureus* (MRSA).
[11] Humans aren't the only ones affected. Antibiotic-resistant bacteria are showing up in penguins waddling across Antarctica, monkeys howling in the deep-dark rainforest, and iguanas lumbering across an island in the Galapagos. How did they get there? No one knows, but human poop goes all kinds of places and carries all kinds of goodies with it.

had to be another answer. And some people would say there was one. But . . . no one was allowed to administer it to her.

That proposed cure wasn't approved by the Food and Drug Administration.[12]

The FDA was struggling to understand this mysterious cure, something called an FMT. Their main question: What was it? A drug? An organ transplant? Or something else completely?

FMT stands for *fecal microbiota transplant*. A doctor proposed that they transplant a healthy microbiome into Lauren's intestines. To do that, they planned to shoot someone else's poop up into her butt.

What?!

That sounded outrageous! The basic idea, though, was nothing new. Back in the fourth century, a Chinese doctor named Ge Hong used stool—administered by mouth!—to cure patients who had food poisoning or severe diarrhea. During World War II, German soldiers in northern Africa noticed sick locals following camels around and eating their steaming stool. Yum-yum. Curious scientists discovered the dung was loaded with a bacterium species, *Bacillus subtilis*, that gobbles other bacteria, including the one that had caused an outbreak of dysentery. Pretty soon the soldiers were slurping stool soup. And my vet said if a bunny has a sick tummy, you feed it poop from a healthy rabbit.

If all the good guys in your gut have been killed off, maybe it makes sense to re-poopulate your gut with someone else's balanced biome.

---

[12] The Food and Drug Administration (FDA) is the US government organization in charge of keeping things safe. They've decided that a jar of peanut butter is "safe" if it has 3 rodent hairs in it but not if it has 4.

Still, this idea sounded pretty far-fetched. I could understand why the FDA was stuck on this decision and insurance companies weren't jumping on board. Lots of doctors didn't even know about the procedure.

But people in pain were desperate for it. With nowhere else to turn, folks started doing it themselves. DIY FMT had become a thing. One guy traveled to Tanzania looking for a "pure" microbiome. He found a donor from a hunter-gatherer tribe, gathered some stool, and used a turkey baster to shoot it up his own bum.

Warning! Warning! Warning! FMTs aren't always safe, particularly when you do it yourself. Diseases such as HIV and hepatitis or parasites might make the leap from one bum to another. Taking your medical care into your own hands isn't necessarily a good thing. Medical professionals worried that sloppy science or sloppy journalism was fanning a dangerous flame.

On the other hand, some medical professionals had been using stool this way for years. In 1957, a medical technologist named Stanley Falkow had people with staph swallow poop. Since the 1980s, Dr. Thomas Borody has done thousands of fecal transplants in Australia. Borody was laughed at. Falkow lost his job. Were they quacks? I doubt their patients thought so. Across the globe, FMTs were helping people, but they still weren't accepted in the US of A.

Then, something happened that changed everything.

In 2013, a paper was published by a team of doctors who cured 81 percent of their *C. diff* patients with fecal transplants! FMTs had cured people before, but all of a sudden, everyone listened. What was different this time? This study was published in the *New England Journal of Medicine*—considered the Holy Grail by many medical professionals. The FDA declared they would treat FMTs as a drug. Now they could make some rules for that drug, and doctors could begin using it in clinical trials.[13]

Back to Lauren's story. No teen in Tennessee had ever had an FMT. After 2 years of the clock *tick-tocking* and the toilet *flish-flushing*, Dr. Maribeth Nicholson got the green light to give it a try. Lauren's brother carried a cup into the restroom and produced the "drug."[14] Dr. Nicholson added some saline, shook it all up,[15] and used a tube to shoot it up into Lauren's rear end.

Using FMTs, doctors are curing *C. diff* infections 80 percent of the time with the first flush and 90 percent with the second flush. For Lauren, the second time was the charm. After 2.5 years of pain, hospitals, blood, and slimy yellow mucus, Lauren won.

C. diff was DONE!

Back in that spick-and-span office at Mount Sinai Hospital, Ari Grinspan bounced on his chair like a kid eager to share a new game. He wanted to show me a fecal transplant from the inside.

He clicked. I leaned. My jaw dropped.

"Oh my gosh!" A river of brown gushed into—not out of—the colon.

"There it is. You just throw it in there. That's it." He slapped his desk.

---

[13] Even the super-screened substance used in clinical trials isn't always safe. One patient died from an antibiotic-resistant bacteria that *came* from his FMT. Sometimes you just can't win.

[14] At that time, doctors used your closest relatives as donors—same food, same environment, similar genes, etc. Nowadays, researchers hypothesize that poop from certain people has more healing power than others. Could your colon be carrying super poo?

[15] Make sure that lid is screwed on tight!

"It looks like vomit," I said. "I mean, going the other direction. Like projectile vomit."

"I put 250 ccs of a fecal slurry inside a colon."

An entire cup of poo. How do you get that into a rectum? A syringe and a lo-o-o-ong nozzle.

This is awesome! I'm thinking that fecal transplants are a silver bullet for *C. difficile,* but then Ari says, "We have a good story. I am re-poopulating the bacteria in your gut from this dysbiotic[16] state, I'm getting you back to health. I can show you that. But is *that* why this works?"

He shakes his head.

"It just works," he says, and no one knows why.

"The other thing is: what else am I giving you with this stuff? All kinds of things. Bacteria, viruses, fungi, and all the products that those microbes make, so I don't know why I can turn this into that, but I can."

Then he plops down a story I don't know how to digest.

In Germany, they did a really intriguing study with 5 patients with *C. diff.* For their FMTs, the doctors used stool that contained no bacteria. No bacteria? How did they manage that? Really, really fine filters.

"All 5 patients," Ari said, "were cured of their *C. diff.* So... Whattt?!"

My brain was scrambling to put those puzzle pieces together. "What we thought was *the* drug in there—"

"This great story of the bacteria re-poopulating the healthy bacteria, well, maybe..." Ari lifts his shoulders in a shrug.

---

[16] *Dys* = bad. *Biotic* = life.

What else could be curing these people? What else was in that stool? Maybe metabolites, the by-products produced by the bacteria? Or viruses (smaller than bacteria, they would have slipped through the filters)?

No one knows, and no one has been able to replicate that study. What's going on? I don't know. Ari doesn't know. No one knows. Yet.

But that mystery isn't holding FMTs back. In fact, they've jumped into fast-forward. Stroll down the street in any major city in America, and you can find a place to get a fecal transplant. Does shooting stool up your backside wig you out? No worries, they've got a pill for that. They call it the crapsule.[17]

There's even a guy planning to make poop-based sports drinks. Would you swig down a slurry from Michael Jordan's you-know-what? It could be teeming with a microbial team to make you an elite athlete! In the stool taken from runners just after a marathon, researchers discovered a spike in one bacterium. That bacterium breaks down lactic acid—the chemical that makes muscles sore and tired. Don't you want some of that? Ultramarathon runners have bacteria that break down carbs and fiber, but Olympic rowers don't. Why? Maybe because ultramarathoners need energy to power through 100 miles. Don't swallow their sales pitch just yet. The studies only show that the bacteria are correlated with these activities, not that the bacteria cause the ultra-performance. Tricky, tricky. Which is it? We need more tests to find out!

Poo-ineers are testing out the gut microbe connections for all

---

[17] A group near Boston pays healthy donors $40 for a stool donation, then proudly provides medical-grade poop to doctors who can order a bottle to go up the bum, a dose to slip down through the nose, or 30 pills to go into the gullet.

sorts of diseases and conditions: allergies, asthma, diabetes, multiple sclerosis, obesity. Drop your finger down anywhere in a medical textbook and you can probably find a microbiome study on that—including the brain: attention-deficit disorder, depression,[18] Parkinson's disease, schizophrenia. Scientists have now labeled the gut our "second brain."

There's even a study on belly bacteria and bullying! Put two male hamsters together and they go at each other—wrestling till one comes up the boss. After the match, the winner and the loser both had fewer *Lactobacillales* (known as a good guy) and more *Clostridioides*! What caused that? The stress of the situation? No one knows yet, but aren't you glad someone's digging deeper to find out?

About one in every 60 kids in America has been diagnosed with autism. They often struggle with behavioral and digestive issues. They also often lack the gut bacterium *Prevotella,* so it should come as no surprise that an FMT could help their tummies, but what about their behaviors? One kid diagnosed with autism had so much trouble in school he wasn't going to pass to the next grade. Then he had an FMT, and his behavior improved so much that he did pass. Did the FMT really do that? That is just *one* anecdote, about *one* boy. Science isn't based on anecdotes. Scientific

---

[18] Feeling down? You could be missing the 2 bacteria recently linked to depression. Or maybe you just need some ice cream.

knowledge isn't built on single stories. But I learned that the boy was part of a scientific study. When 18 autistic kids were given FMTs, both their digestive and their behavioral issues improved. Their hyperactivity and their repetitive actions decreased. Just think about how many lives FMTs might change!

And FMTs aren't reserved for two-leggeds.

With their button eyes, froofy ears, and fur so fleecy your fingers want to plunge in, koalas are adorable! But koalas have a problem—they are picky eaters. Strike everything from their menu except eucalyptus leaves. And even with hundreds of different kinds of eucalyptus to choose from, some koalas will eat only one species. That's setting themselves up for a fall.

Koalas who crunch through all the leaves of their chosen eucalyptus in their home range can starve—even if there's a whole forest of another eucalyptus standing right in front of them. Why won't they branch out? Maybe it's their microbes.

Researcher Ben Moore discovered those who eat the manna gum eucalyptus had different microbes in their droppings than those who ate the messmate eucalyptus. Ben made up some poo pills and transplanted microbes from one koala to another. After that, some koalas could eat both kinds of eucalyptus. This could save their lives![19] Could fecal transplants be a silver bullet for saving endangered species?

This little procedure, and the idea of mighty microbes, has turned our understanding of what's healthy on its head. It has helped change our entire perspective—all of a sudden, *bacteria* isn't a bad

---

[19] Koalas aren't safe yet. Although they *could* eat the new leaves, some of those cuties still said, "No way!"

word. For decades, we have tried so hard to kill those little microbes. Now, science says we should go play in the dirt (just don't eat it).

As I'm writing this, my kitty, Annie, leaps to my lap, looking for a nap. But my knees are bouncing with energy. *Prrrrp!* Annie complains on the way back down. She just doesn't get how cool this is! Stool saving human—and animal—lives!

She finds a puddle of sunshine and curls up for a snooze. Watching her belly rise and fall, I imagine the microbes munching away in her pretty pink colon.[20] What other miracles, I wonder, do these rainforests-within-us hold? And what might happen if we let microbial species go extinct?

---

[20] One day, I mailed Annie's stool to AnimalBiome. A month later I got a file full of colorful graphs and pie charts showing me her microbiome. When I saw *Clostridia* listed, I freaked out, but then I actually read the info and discovered that plenty of *Clostridia* species are good guys. The AnimalBiome researchers found 13 new types of bacteria in the stool of one cat, the internet celebrity Lil Bub. Cool!

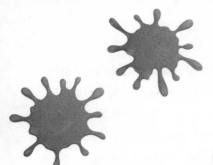

CHAPTER 8
MORE FECES, PLEASE!

Poop in the water—in the toilet, in the river, in the pool? That's just nasty. Normally, we flush it away and the problem's gone. Well, one stinkin' hot day when I stood beside a fishpond covered in bellies turned up, there was no way to flush those problems away. They flopped right in front of my face.

The cows mooing behind me hadn't meant to be murderers, but their derrieres were the smoking—or should I say steaming—guns. Well-managed cattle drop their dung far from the water, but then gravity grabs it and—with an assist from H_2O—sloshes it on down into the pond.

Algae think cow pies are delicious! Not really. Algae don't eat pies; they photosynthesize. But in the game of life, algae need nitrogen. And cow pies are full of that.

Nitrogen (N) is the MVP of the nutrient world, but he's kind of an odd fellow. He's everywhere. The air around you is 78 percent nitrogen, yet plants die because they can't get enough. See, most of the N in the air is in the wrong form, N_2, like a movie in the wrong file format. Some plants have superstar bacteria on their roots that convert N_2 to a usable form, but most don't. They have to wait around on something else to contribute usable nitrogen to the soil.[1] But give those daisies a scoop of poop and watch them dance!

Nitrogen is such a big deal that carnivorous plants kill for it.[2]

Nitrogen. Nitrogen! NITROGEN! Every living thing wants nitrogen. Why? Plants need it for that little thing called photosynthesis.[3] Chlorophyll is the star player in the photosynthesis game. And every chlorophyll needs 4 nitrogen atoms at its core. No nitrogen? No plants. No plants? No people.

Oh, and every A, T, C, or G of DNA is built on nitrogen, too.

So, when all that N washes into the fishpond, it's like a party with nitrogen nachos! Algae grow and grow until the pond is so thick, you think you can walk right across it. But every party's got

---

[1] That "something else" could be freewheeling bacteria, a dead body, or lightning. Nitrogen in the atmosphere is actually 2 atoms clinging tight as N_2. When lightning zaps them apart, they bond with oxygen and get on with becoming useful to life.

[2] Most pitcher plants get their N by killing insects, but one in Borneo has a better idea. She turns her body into a toilet. Instead of waiting for insects to fall into her pitcher-shaped trap, she invites in a woolly bat. The bat gets a clean place to sleep, then pays the plant with nitrogen-laden poop.

[3] Poop fertilizer is such a big deal that a zoo in Seattle runs a lottery for it. Aren't you dying to win a truckload of Zoo Doo for your garden?

to end, and when the N runs out, that's the end of algae. No one's crying over dying algae, but their dead bodies feed bacteria. And here's where things get dicey for the fish. In a small pond, there's only so much oxygen to go around. The bacteria ball hogs suck it all up. With no oxygen, it's bye-bye fishies. ☹

And that's how cow pies turned the pond I was staring at into a kettle of dead bodies. It didn't seem right. I mean, the land needed the nitrogen. Just to get the grass to grow, that farmer had to spray chicken manure on his pasture every year. But this? The pale bellies swirled slowly, like empty rafts at a water park on a stormy day. It seemed like the system should have been better designed than that.

I knew all that from reading, but I wanted to understand how feces actually turns into fertilizer. It decomposes, but how? And when? And by whom?

Down in Costa Rica, scientist Nancy Greig and her students had those same kinds of questions, so they each placed a brownie-sized dollop of human poo onto the forest floor, then squatted to watch. Their first visitors? Flesh flies—bugs who know the feces are fleeting, so they don't mess around. They skip laying eggs like normal insects and give birth to maggots already squirming and ready to munch. Down in those steamy tropics, poo didn't even last a day.

I also wanted to know: is it different if it's a cow's or mine or Piper's or some wild animal's? So, one day when I found a mysterious scat, tar black and twisted, I plopped it down right beside Piper's. Then we'd check it every day on our morning walk.

Day after day, Piper's just sat there like a gloopy cow splat. Nothing happening. Not so with the black scat. By Day 3, someone had wiggled it into a different position. By Day 5, rain had rinsed it, revealing an orange center and persimmon seeds. I thought of the poop tea seeping into the soil, steeping the plant roots in life-giving nutrients.

Then, on Day 13, a long, large slug sprawled across the dark, damp mound. Gliding along, his head ducked under a 2-cm chestnut-colored ledge. My knees damp with dew, my loupe to my eye, I was so close the swirls on his back stood out like the ridges on my fingerprint. This slug was in heaven. Me, too.

A slug eats with thousands of teeth on a ribbonlike band called a radula. It works like a tongue. Imagine sliding belly-down across scat, licking it like an ice cream cone. Animals that survive on poop blow my mind. The ultimate recyclers! But where do those nutrients go from there? It can't stop with a slug.

On the internet I found some German folks who discovered how a slug acts like a bus. Sometimes slugs swallow mites.[4] Of the mites that get ingested, 70 percent don't get digested, so they get egested (whole) in the feces. They're dumped into a new home up to 4 meters away from where they hopped onto the slug bus. To a tall two-legged, 4 m might not sound like a long way, but it is 2,000 times farther than those creepy crawlies could trek on their own.

Poop transportation? Is that a thing? I started Googling and found a story on a whole different scale—a whale-sized scale.

I met with Dr. Joe Roman over Skype. One of the first times he ever saw a right whale,[5] he got more than a glimpse of the planet's rarest large whale; he got a bonus—a massive plume of poo.

---

[4] A mite? Think: a spider relative who looks like a watermelon seed with legs but is so small you need a magnifying glass to spy on him.

[5] Right whales got their name because people said they were the "right" whale to hunt. We killed so many, they almost went extinct.

Right whale feces are as orange as a pumpkin. Clumps bob along the surface, then dissolve and sink as a dusty swirl. Imagine the bowel movement of a 70-ton animal. And the smell? Greasy. Joe says you'll never wash it out of your clothes.[6]

That image of the whale and the feces plume stuck in Joe's mind as he went through school, learning about how animals move nutrients around. Animals like super-shaggy sloths that creep down their tree once a day to poop, planting nutrients right where they can be used.[7] Joe also learned about the biological pump.

Just like in the pond, when teeny tiny ocean algae called phytoplankton run out of nutrients, they stop growing. Some get eaten; others die and sink. The nutrients in their bodies (nitrogen, phosphorus, and carbon) can get carried down, down, down, all the way to the sea floor, where they get eaten or buried in gunk.

Phytoplankton are the base of the ocean food chain. Without them, all the albatross, barracuda, corals, dolphins, and almost every other living ocean creature would starve. I think about the anchovies, blue crabs, clams, and every other fishy food I eat. Think of how many humans depend on the ocean for food. If phytoplankton disappeared, though, starving wouldn't be our first issue. Breathing would.

Phytoplankton produce 20 percent of the oxygen on the planet. Every fifth breath you take, you should thank the phyto.

---

[6] Poonado: Spinning in its own poop, a sperm whale created a 30-meter-wide swirlie. The divers watching it got a once-in-a-lifetime experience—whale poo in their wetsuits, their eyes, even their mouths!

[7] Sloths s-l-o-w-l-y descend to do their business at the base of a tree. Why not just let it drop? Maybe to make sure it fertilizes the right tree. Another hypothesis: to give moth eggs a nice nursery. The adult moths live in the sloth's fur and fertilize algae living in there. The sloths gain extra nutrition by eating the algae. When sloths visit the ground, mama moths lay their eggs in the protective poop. Later, caterpillars climb aboard their new mobile home.

Joe knew a lot about phytoplankton and the biological pump—the way nutrients cycle downward. What he didn't know was that one day his brain would connect that pump idea with the whale feces he had seen. On that day, Joe came up with a mega idea totally new to science.

"I realized that whales were actually doing the opposite thing," Joe said. "They are diving down to feed and then they come to the surface, where they rest, they digest, and then they also defecate."

Whales were cycling nutrients back up to start the whole process over again.

That was a big moment. So big, he still keeps the drawing he made in his notebook that day.

But an "Aha" moment doesn't prove anything. "Sure, there's some nutrients that get to the surface," one scientist told him, "but is it biologically or ecologically important? Or is it a fart in a hurricane?"

To answer those questions, Joe had to quantify his idea. He had to nail some numbers onto each of those nutrients. With calculator and computer and lots of head scratching, a team modeled the system, made their best estimates, and pounded the numbers out. How much do whales eat? Excrete? Move? What's the amount of nitrogen? Phosphorus? Iron?

Their results were pretty impressive. Based on their calculations there in the Gulf of Maine, it looked like the whales might be dumping in as many nutrients as all the rivers in the area combined.

"Wow!" I said. "That's got to be important."

Joe thought it was. He even gave this idea a name: the whale pump. But other scientists challenged him: you haven't actually gone out and measured it. Joe needed evidence.

So, his team jumped into a boat and went to trail some whales. Think of a crew of scientists bobbing in a boat with long-handled nets at the ready and binoculars to their eyes. I imagined them calling out: *Here, whalie-whalie-whalies!* Then Joe told me they actually joined another project that used suction-cup tags to track whales. They got to follow individual whales all day.[8]

And indeed, they found very high levels of nitrogen in those feces.

So, that means Joe's idea was right!

Well, Joe explained, what it really means is, "The evidence is there, and now we have a hypothesis that can be tested."

"In science," he went on, "rarely do you get a yes or a no. It's not unusual for the first scientific study to be flashy, to say, 'wow, this is huge!'" And then other scientists come in with different results or interpretations. Other scientists repeat the study to see if the results are reliable; that is, they come out the same way even with a different population of whales, in another ocean, etc.

But this whole whale pump idea did make a splash. Keeping our phytoplankton abundant and healthy is a really big deal.

I'm thinking about how brave it is to put your idea out there into the world for people to chop up. Joe's worrying about how whales are being chopped up.

"There are only about 500 North Atlantic right whales on the planet. One of the most endangered species in the world." His voice, which has been hard science and square numbers, becomes soft and round.

---

[8] One whale study in the icy Antarctic sends drones to do the dirty work. Smart!

Most schools have more than 500 students.

"And we've lost..." A sigh seeps from his chest. "I think the latest number is 17—to blunt force trauma or fishing entanglements." Whales get hit by ships or wrapped up in fishing gear.

"Entangled, it's so hard to feed, hard to migrate, hard to breathe. So painful. The gashes are going right in through the blubber, down to the muscle." I flinch at that.

And with every one of those gashes, every one of those deaths, the ocean loses a whale pumping nutrients back into the cycle.

With his focus on feces, Joe had gone beyond uncovering the story of an individual coyote, beyond recovering the story of a koala population. Joe was discovering the power of poop to keep an entire ecosystem chugging.

Right whales aren't the only ones doing the right thing to help the ocean. Gray whales, blue whales, and humpback whales are part of the whale pump, too. And megamammals aren't the only megamovers. Penguins eat in the ocean, waddle up on land to nest and—splat! One colony made such a huge mess it was spotted from space! And that colony with 1.5 million Adélie penguins had never been discovered before. They had hidden successfully till a computer program scanning satellite images caught their dark, dirty mess. *Bing-bing-bing!* Guano gave them away![9]

When seabirds roost on a rocky island, there's so much white guano that the island looks like an iceberg. Seabirds contribute ~591

---

[9] In another penguin study, 1.5 million volunteers scanned through 175,000 penguin pics to help scientists make a discovery. Wherever penguins poop, snow melted faster. Hmm... dark feces would soak up more sunlight than white snow would. Maybe penguins use their poop to prepare a good nest site.

gigagrams[10] of nitrogen to the ocean each year. And 15–20 percent of the nitrogen in coral comes from bird guano. Every little Nemo (and other coral-dwelling critter) should be glad for bird guano.[11]

By the end of my chat with Joe, I was bouncing in my chair. Look at what poo can do!

Not long afterward, a headline about an upside to poop in the river caught my attention. Poop getting more good press? Yes! I was off like a dog after a deer. My keyboard and mouse chased that story up over the Atlantic, across the dry desert, and down to the bank of the Mara River in Kenya, Africa. There, the Maasai people kept seeing batches of fish floating by belly up, and everyone wanted to know who killed the fish!

About 4,000 pudgy, crinkle-necked, blunt-nosed hippos live along the Mara River. In the dark of the night, hippos munch leaves on land. In the heat of the day, they loll around in cool pools and do their business. As you might guess, hippos can produce prodigious amounts of poop, dumping ~18,739 pounds per day into the river. Business as usual.

Normally all their "stuff" sinks to the bottom. With all that, there's probably not much oxygen left down there, but no one seems to mind. Occasionally, though, there's a

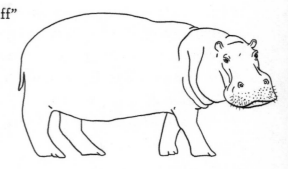

---

[10] That number means nothing to me, so I convert it to pounds: 1,302,931,969.5 lbs. Then to US tons: 651,466. That's still just a big number. Finally, I figured a way to comprehend it. That weight is equal to over 400,000 hippos.

[11] Back in the 1800s, European farmers were glad, too. Their land was so starved for nutrients that they hauled in guano from islands off the coast of Peru. By 1844, one small island had produced 450 ships' worth and had shrunk by 25 feet!

super heavy rain. All that H_2O flushes the feces-rich, oxygen-poor water downstream . . .

A scientific team sent a robotic boat in to test the nitrogen and oxygen levels in the water.[12] Yep. The hippo hypothesis was confirmed. Death due to doo-doo. So, why were they claiming it was a good thing? Because this is a natural cycle. This cycle helps things balance out. Without it, fish populations might grow like crazy. Besides, everybody downstream needs that nitrogen. Plus, when those fish die, birds and crocs get a free feast. The team found that the fish kills happened 9 times in 5 years, and each time, the natural system took it in stride.

Once scientists saw things bounce back in the Mara, they wondered if other rivers needed this, too. What if this flush of nutrients is normal?

Megamunchers move mega-amounts of nutrients through their poo. Whales were doing it in the ocean. Hippos were doing it in the river. What about other ecosystems?

As this stuff was blowing my mind, I read an article titled "Global Nutrient Transport in a World of Giants" that Joe Roman had helped with. It plopped down another mega idea. Maybe we've not yet understood the importance of these cycles—the whale pump, the hippo dump—because our modern world is missing a few megapoopers.

Think of those that used to roam the earth: the dinosaurs! And I'm not talking about a puny turd or two from *Tyrannosaurus rex*. No meat eater can compete with the massive output of an herbivore. I'm talking somebody like *Patagotitan mayorum*.[13] A dinosaur with

---

[12] They had to dress it up to look like a crocodile so the hippos wouldn't charge it.
[13] Never heard of him? That's because this titanosaur was just discovered.

an escalator neck who nibbled off entire treetops. The heaviest dino ever. He weighed as much as the space shuttle! Just think of all the nutrients he and all his buddies spread around. When we lost him and all his crew, the earth lost all that fertile feces.

Even if you look back just 12,000 years, at the end of the last Ice Age, there were 48 mega-plant munchers. Today, only 9 of those are left standing: 3 elephants, 5 rhinos, and the mighty hippo.

In modern times, some spots in Africa might be able to stand up to their prehistoric poop potential, but Africa's got elephants, giraffes, and rhinos. The rest of the world? Not so much. South America has lost all 15 of its megamunchers[14] and now stands at less than 0.01 percent of its fecal capacity.[15]

In today's game, who can swagger up to the plate and produce? We better save every single hippo. Every single elephant. Every single whale.

We need more feces!

---

[14] A few of their vanished giants: glyptodons, which looked like armadillos the size of a sedan; giant ground sloths twice as tall as humans; and *Argentinosaurus*, whose femur (thigh bone) was 2.35 m long.

[15] Should we bring back extinct species like mammoths to re-wild our world? Some people think so. Others shudder at the idea.

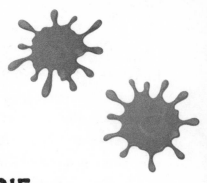

CHAPTER 9
PUMPKIN PIE

When I was a little kid, like 4 years old, my dad used to keep me busy by giving me *x* and *y* coordinates to graph on a piece of chart paper. Yes, those graphs you do in math class. And I *loved* it! I had to puzzle out each variable, count up the little lines, and figure out just where to put the dot. Then, once I had 5 or 10 done, he'd tell me to connect the dots. It was like magic. From random dots, suddenly a picture appeared!

That's how this story went. I was bumbling along, finding lots of little dots of info that were cool and all, but . . . Then I put them all together—okay, I admit I needed Dr. Logan Kistler to connect the dots for me—and something unexpected was staring me in the face.

Dr. Kistler is a curator of archaeobotany and archaeogenomics at the Smithsonian National Museum of Natural History. Honestly, I don't know much about archaeology let alone his super-specialized specialties, but when we get on the phone to chat, I discover he's super nice and down to earth and can explain things in ways I understand. Pretty soon, we are on a first-name basis.

I was telling him a story: "So, there's this scientist, Dr. Henry Greene, dissecting rattlesnakes from the Mojave Desert, and he finds seeds in their guts." Logan's like, "What?" Even though I can't see him sitting in his office in the bowels of the museum some 700 miles away from me, I can almost hear him lean into the story. Everyone knows rattlesnakes don't eat seeds. Well, we never thought they ate seeds, but slicing open a rattler's belly, Dr. Greene had found a different set of evidence. I'm imagining Logan putting the variables of this story together in his head: rattlers eat rodents (chipmunks, mice, etc.), rodents pack seeds in their pouches, so . . .

"And the cool thing is," I gush on, "he mapped it out, and the snakes are dispersing the seeds way farther than the rodents would have, and because it is a reptile—"

"Oh!"

From the tone of his voice, I can tell this scientist is as intrigued by the story as I am. That makes me happy.

Dispersal is all about how a seed is carried across the landscape, and Logan had also made a startling discovery about seed dispersal. His discovery wasn't about dandelion seeds dancing on the wind or crafty coconuts bobbing on the waves. His discovery was much more complex than that. His discovery was more similar to these super-sneaky grass seeds squirreled away in a chipmunk's pouches and then kerplatted down in a new place to grow. So, he probably knew that between the chomping and the gut enzymes, seeds don't always make it through a rodent's guts (or a human's, for that matter). But if a snake gulps down a chipper before that munk has a chance to munch, if the seeds are still snug in those mouth pouches, there's not much in a snake's gut designed to attack those seeds.

"Some of the seeds," I add, "were *germinating* inside of the snakes."

"That is pretty wild!" Logan exclaims.

A seed is happiest in soil that's dark, damp, and full of nutrients. And out in the dry, sandy desert, a snake gut is probably the darkest, dampest, most nutrient-rich place going. When those conditions are just right, a seed gets ready to pop open, to germinate. But it takes time. The GPT, or "gut passage time," of a sidewinder rattler? Just so happens to be 11 to 24 days. Time enough for a seed to get a start. It's like snakes are the perfect seed incubators!

Point 1: *Plink!* The variables for the first point on our graph are snakes and seeds. Snakes on one axis, seeds on the other, and voila, we have seed dispersal, our first little black dot.

When two life forms live closely together like this, it's called symbiosis. Symbiosis stories always suck me in. It's like two little whirlwinds tugging at my mind, and I can't resist trying to figure out their puzzle. All three types of symbiosis are cool:

- Parasitism, where a bad guy steals from a good guy (think: a tiny tick-like mite slurps blood from the legs of an unsuspecting daddy longlegs).
- Commensalism, where one organism gets something good out of the deal and the other one isn't affected much (think: seeds and rattlesnakes).
- Mutualism, a thumbs-up for both organisms. Even more intricate, that is the kind of symbiosis Dr. Kistler had discovered in dung.

To find our second graph point on our imaginary graph, we need to go back to last Thanksgiving. My family is gathered at tables scattered all around the house. I'm at the kids' table because that's where the laughter is. I raise a bite of pumpkin pie to my mouth and say a silent thank-you. A thank-you to the farmer who grew the wheat, the sailors who shipped the cinnamon, the inventor who made it possible to extract the salt,[1] the cow who donated the milk (probably unwillingly), and the mastodon who provided the pumpkin.

You read that right. Every Thanksgiving, we should thank those ancient elephant-relatives.

Stare up at megasized tusks in a museum, and you will wonder just how a mastodon could have anything to do with pumpkin pie.

Two days earlier, I had been baking the pumpkin pie, with all those savory scents wafting around me. It almost burned, though, because my nose was buried in an article. An article about scientists who had connected the dots in a picture of pumpkins, taste buds, and ancient poo.

Dr. Logan Kistler and his colleague Dr. Lee Newsom had dug up a wet wad of mastodon dung from an ancient sinkhole in Florida.[2] Mastodons were herbivores. No surprise that in the 12,000-year-old dung deposit, the scientists found some seeds mixed in with the snipped twigs, leaves, fruits, and other mastodon munch.

Point 2: Mastodons and dung. *Plink!*

"I reckon there's probably hundreds of seeds from a couple of sites," said Logan. "So, this is a regular thing."

When he says "regular," he's not talking about avoiding

---

[1] Cinnamon is harvested directly from tree bark, but salt has to be: (1) chiseled out of the ground by human-operated machines, (2) scooped out of shallow ponds where the sun has done some evaporation work, or (3) sucked out of the earth as a salty brine and then separated from water by an elaborate vacuum evaporation system.

[2] The ancient poo wasn't as hardened as you'd expect. The sinkhole is currently under a river, so sometimes the team had to scuba dive down to the poo. What did it smell like? Only a scientist like Dr. Kistler would provide this description: "vaguely anaerobic [a process that requires the absence of oxygen] and muddy."

constipation. The reason this "regular thing" plops a big black dot into our picture is because the seeds were from wild gourds. In his paper, Logan had written that these plants produce "a cytotoxic suite of cucurbitacins—harshly bitter triterpenoid compounds." Translation: gourds concoct chemicals to kill the cells of animals that eat them.

Point 3: Bitter and killer. Those chemicals are the most bitter naturally occurring compound.

"Have you tried it?" I asked him.

Yup, but it was an accident. One day after working with some wild gourds, Logan took a break for lunch. "I had washed my hands and everything, but it [the chemical] transferred to the food I was eating. Uggg." Not a pleasant bitter, like dark chocolate. "It is *really* gross. You've got to spit it right out." And those nasty cytotoxins aren't limited to gourds. "Even a cucumber, if you get one that is a bit green and mushy, can still express this gene pathway."[3]

Now, don't use this as an excuse to go skipping your veggies. Unless you can't taste bitter things, a person could never eat enough cucumber to be fatal.

"Bitter taste perception is an adaptive response to avoiding poison," Logan explains.

I stop him right there because I've heard you are supposed to eat bitter foods because they are oh so healthy. There's a whole genus of plants related to mustards that are bitter but not capital-*B* bitter. Cabbage, broccoli, Brussels sprouts—yep, the ones you might love to hate—which can help prevent cancer.[4]

Logan tells me that some bitter plants have been used to get

---

[3] Two women in France lost their hair from the same chemicals in squash!

[4] Don't love them? The folks at the National Mustard Museum say, Go guzzle some mustard. They claim mustard seed fights cancer too.

rid of parasites, "As in you are poisoning your parasites more than you are yourself."

Later, I found an article about how people in Mexico and China gobbled down pumpkin seeds when they had a tapeworm. Those long skinny ribbons use grappling hooks on their heads to grab your gut lining and hang on. The 15-foot thieves mooch your food right through their skin. Imagine the relief if you could send one of those guys packing thanks to a pumpkin.

But what does any of this have to do with mastodons? And snakes carrying seeds?

Point 4: Pumpkins and gourds. Pumpkins wouldn't exist if mastodons hadn't pooped the wild gourd seeds.

Pumpkins belong to the genus *Cucurbita*; their great-great-great-great-granddaddies are wild gourds. Back before people were around, wild gourd plants would pop up helter-skelter across the North American landscape. Well, it might seem helter-skelter, but map it out and you would find (like the pumpkin plants in my compost) they preferred sunny spots, places that have been recently churned up, where they don't have much tree competition. Just the kind of place that's left behind after a massive mammal has trampled through the forest and taken a dump.

How could mastodons eat toxic gourds? Logan explains. If miniature mammals (like mice, marsh rats, or elephant shrews[5]) munched on the gourds, they'd kick the bucket. But if megamammals (like mastodons, mammoths, or elephants) munched and crunched, no problem.

---

[5] With a long snout perfected for probing soil and a flick-happy tongue, elephant shrews go about their day lapping up insects and crunching through the occasional worm. But maybe they've read all those healthy diet magazines, because they are known to swallow plant shoots and fruits.

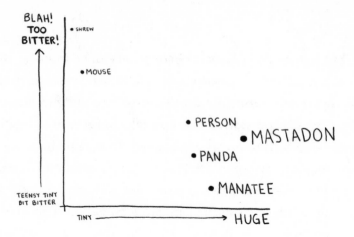

How come?

Thanks to the fact that large animals eat a lot, a drip-drop of toxin might very well zip right on through their gut (without being absorbed) and then splat out the other end. Or if it does get sucked in by their system, it might be diluted enough not to faze them.[6]

Point 5: Toxin and taste buds. Mastodons couldn't taste bitter flavors.

Logan sleuthed his way into the genes and discovered that other large herbivores don't taste bitter either. Whereas something small like a common shrew has 38 genes telling its tongue to scream if something bitter enters its lips, a huge animal like a West Indian manatee has only 8.

"We found a beautiful correlation," Logan said, his voice rising in excitement. "It was as lucky as I ever got with a science thing."

Did you catch that he said *correlation*, not *causation*? To a scientific brain, that word is like a flashing yellow light. When two things are correlated, it means they are related in some way. All too often, folks make the mistake of thinking it means one *caused* the

---

[6] We can't go cramming poison down a mastodon's throat, but we can see that it would take 75–230 wild gourds to kill an African elephant. Even stuffing them in like a mouthful of mini marshmallows, an elephant couldn't manage that many.

other, but it doesn't. Finding a correlation can be important (it may even lead us to find a causation), but watch out for those tricksters.[7]

Nevertheless, scientific predictions rarely come out as clean as that. Logan's correlation was something for him to be proud of, but I am wondering, *So what*? I mean, this stuff happened eons ago and mastodons are extinct. This story's dead and done, right?

If you are Logan Kistler, you get just what an intricate mutualistic relationship this was. The mastodons get food planted for the future, and gourds get planted in a perfectly sunny spot. If you are Logan Kistler, you are thinking about the massive ecosystem changes that happened once mastodons go extinct and no longer roam the landscape. If you are Logan Kistler, a little nudge reminds you that at just about that time, another species was coming onto the landscape . . .

Homo sapiens.

"Essentially the disappearance of megafauna, coupled with the arrival of humans, pushed humans and wild squashes into the landscape together. And then it was just a matter of selection and several thousand years of tinkering . . ."

What was that tinkering? Someone long, long ago must have found a wild squash that was not quite as bitter as the rest. She planted its seeds and grew it like crazy. She picked the least bitter of those fruits and planted those seeds. Pick, plant, repeat a couple thousand times. And voila, that may be how humans domesticated the pumpkin.[8]

Point 6: People and pumpkins. Which is all well and good, but

---

[7] If Piper's poop was runny on every Monday, I shouldn't assume it was runny *because* the calendar said *Monday*. Maybe it was because she got treats from my table on Sunday.
[8] Or, how the pumpkin domesticated humans.

if gourds had gone kaput, and we had to do without pumpkin pie, we would survive, right? He's put all these dots on the graph, but I can't see the big deal.

Then Logan says something that makes my brain do a backflip.

"We get *all* of our calories from domestic species."

Oh. Understanding this story of where pumpkins came from might be important. I've been looking back, back, back through a time machine telescope to zoom in on what I thought was simply a giggle-inducing pumpkin poo story. I've been focusing on each and every little dot. Logan, on the other hand, is connecting the dots to see a bigger picture.

"It's worth thinking about their long-term evolutionary/ecology context." He pauses to let that sink in.

My mind starts churning on all that was required to get just one kind of food, the pumpkin. It took an extremely long time. It took not one, but two mutualistic relationships: gourds and mastodons plus people and pumpkins. It took coevolution—the process of where organisms influence each other as they both change through time.

I blink and connect the dots on my imaginary graph.

The picture is a fork.

And this is when the whole story starts to get personal. This story is about food. *My* food. And all that food, I suddenly realize, is the result of intricate interactions between multiple organisms.

Logan says, there's looking at where your food comes from (like the store or the tree or the country where cinnamon is grown), and then there is looking at where your food *really* comes from.

Huh.

His research is about the "deep time" story of our food—the

story of food across the entire span of the earth's past—and poop gives us clues into that.

Then, Dr. Logan Kistler turns our time machine toward the future. He has a few concerns. "Specifically when we have climate change, ecological change, the pressures of a growing population..."

Each of those pose threats to the future of our food.

Up to this point, my questions have been about the cool clues you collect from an animal's rear end. But the picture Logan has drawn points to the other end. Now it's like I am staring down a black hole that runs right through my own body. It all leads me to wonder: what does the poop of today mean for the future?

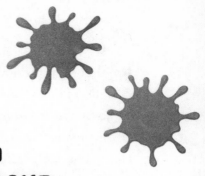

CHAPTER 10
ALPHABET SOUP

Thank goodness for Kat Black. Kat is finding answers about food and the future using poop. Not cat poop (I know her name could fool you) or people poop, but poop from the red fox—one of the coolest canines I know. I mean, the coolest *wild* canine[1] (my apologies, Piper).

That's why I was surprised by her Skype profile picture. It wasn't a red fox. It wasn't fox tracks or even fox feces. It was Kat squatting on smooth sand, the cool blue of sea and sky behind her. Her sleeves rolled up, a braid draped over her shoulder, her hands cupped around something small and gray.

Once we connected, laptop to laptop, my first question was, "Were you holding a sea turtle egg?" I imagined her on some isolated Caribbean island. The places she's gone for research—Madagascar with its oh-so-awesome lemurs and a few diseases, the Sierra Nevada Mountains with jaw-dropping views and avalanches that like to swallow scientists whole—are so amazing and gnarly she didn't tell her mom about them until she was safely back home.

---

[1] But then again I also love painted wolves . . . sigh. When scientists needed to keep two packs of painted wolves apart, they built a poop fence. Sure the wolves could have jumped over, but the smell told them to stay out of that territory.

"No, that's a piping plover chick."

"Oh." Did I have the wrong Kat Black?

But soon she was telling me all about her fox study out on Fire Island, off the coast of New York.

"For foxes, we really have no idea what they do on barrier islands," she said. As it turns out, foxes haven't been on Fire Island forever. No one knows when they came or how they came.[2] No one knows what they are eating, where they are living, or what their island life is like.

"So, I guess my dissertation research is looking at closing a lot of those scientific knowledge gaps."

Scat to the rescue! Kat's study is part of a larger study about how animal populations on Fire Island are interacting. A study that could give data to land managers who are facing a dilemma. You see, some people have been asking: does the fox belong on Fire Island?

Thinking back to my bat guano puzzle, I am eager to hear how Kat made sense from the bits and pieces in scat. Unlike a tracker following a tidy line of tracks to get to know one animal intimately, Kat follows transect lines to get to know an entire population.

"We overlaid the whole island with a 300-meter grid map and divided it up, creating these straight-line transects. Every time we walk these transects, we'll kind of put on our poop goggles."[3]

Collecting samples along those fixed lines, Kat can get a valid representation of the feces. It sure would be easier to pick up the

---

[2] Did they swim across? Hitchhike with some humans? Trot on over when the water was low? Who knows!

[3] In real life, the lines aren't 100 percent straight. Her crew almost mutinied when she wanted them to bushwack through a poison ivy forest.

convenient scats, but those might all be from foxes who hang out by a dumpster—a foxy version of a convenience store. That would certainly bias her study. With a valid set of samples, she can estimate results for the entire fox population without combing every inch of the island on hands and knees.

I was dying to put on my own poop goggles and walk those transects, too. So, I made plans to join Kat the following fall. But that summer, the foxes got mange;[4] the population plummeted; Kat wasn't going to be collecting. After 10 months of waiting, I was raring to go, though, so I went without her.

Fire Island was so cool! Sprawled on the sand, there was a dino-sized bone. In the visitor center, there was a hunk of something that felt like whiskers from a giant's face but was baleen from a whale's mouth. On the trail behind a dune, I fingered a dip in the sand. A fox print? My radar went up.

My eyes patrolled the trail ahead. My nose caught the spicy scent of bayberry. The trail dumped me into a river of sand that ran all the way across the island—from the Atlantic on my left to Bellport Bay on my right. You'd think that was a long way, but right there the island was only 0.2 of a mile across. A ranger told me hurricanes carry waves up over the dunes and wash clear across the island sometimes. They dumped fresh sand and coconuts from foreign lands. They also cleared out the vegetation and made my job easier.

Little divots in the sand had me ping-ping-pinging around in anticipation. Were they tracks? Would they lead to scat?

---

[4] Sarcoptic mange is caused by tiny parasitic mites—house guests who tunnel into the fox's skin, where they dump eggs and feces. The itch can be so bad, some foxes have chewed off their own tails. ☹

There—where the land lay low and the sand was hard packed—a line of neat prints. I feel the trotting motion of that fox moving toward the bay. My hands moved with her paws, then paused. There, just to the right, another line of tracks. Neat tracks. Petite tracks. Tracks that just might be a fox kit. Five minutes later, I came upon three small chunks—hard, dark, and crusted with salt-and-pepper sand. Scat! Where is Kat? I want to show her my find!

Who does that belong to? Dog? Coyote? Raccoon? Gray fox? I could stick-pick my way through it; I could take clues from the perforated line of tracks in the sand; I could even measure each turd down to the nth decimal place, but I was left with just guesses. Every flip through the field guide gave me too many options: Skunk? Cat? Or maybe, just maybe, red fox?

"No matter how good you are at identifying tracks and scat in the field," Kat had told me, "there is no way to be 100 percent certain what it came from." After 2 years of collecting, she's got a whole library of scat. How does she know whose is whose?

Some days she gets lucky. Kat's literally stood there and watched a fox scat. Imagine that!

"They'll look you in the eye and are like, 'You watching me?' And then I'm like, 'Should I give you some space? I just want to, uh, collect that.'"

How did she ever get that close? Was she some kind of fox whisperer? Well, the wildlife on Fire Island isn't exactly "wild." I watched a young couple

handing out corn chips to 4 deer in the middle of a parking lot. This habitat is home to lots of two-leggeds who are on vacation.

Most of the time, to know whose poo it is, Kat relies on super-sleuthing through the alphabet soup of DNA. Those 4 bases—**a**denine, **t**hymine, **g**uanine, and **c**ytosine—line up in a long, long string, like:

atgtctgggcagggccccagagaaggctgctggg ctctcccaatgccacctccccaacc[5]

Sure, we humans use that code for detective work, but the real purpose of those magical letters is to spell out a recipe, telling the cell what proteins to make. Those proteins determine the specific features of an organism.

I want to know what's behind the "Abracadabra!" of DNA extraction.

Turns out, it takes a little grit. After her field season, Kat loads up a cooler and carts her treasures back to the lab at Virginia Tech. Just like HJ, she needs to track down those runaway epithelial cells. Unlike HJ, Kat's got tracks to follow. Other scientists have already learned how to extract fox DNA.

Sitting in her lab, Kat pointed her pen at the end of a 2-inch turd in a plastic tube. The pointy part on the end is a great place to find those epithelial cells. And inside those cells, she'll find the DNA she's after.[6]

What Kat needs to know—did this DNA come from a red

---

[5] This particular sequence is from the stretch of code that determines if fox fur is orange or black. It's turned "on" in fur of the feet, tail, ears—anywhere the fox is black. It is silenced anywhere the fur is carrot colored.

[6] There's tons of DNA on the inside of the turd, too, but that's DNA from the food, not the fox.

fox?—is lurking in the mitochondrial DNA.[7] She sends it off to a lab where they do a couple of procedures and eventually get a text file that looks like gobbledygook. Armed with a section of 400 mumbo-jumbo A's, T's, G's, or C's from the sample, they compare it to the code from known samples: dog, raccoon, gray fox, etc. When the sample matches the code for red fox, Kat's got a winner!

Staring down at those three turds on Fire Island, I felt like a winner, too. Could this scat give me some answers? Could it close some of the gaps in my scientific knowledge?

I grabbed a clam's shell, let my knees sink into the soft sand, and started sawing.

The inside was the color of cooked sausage. My loupe on my eye, I entered the magnified world of a turd. Hair. Ultrafine, gray, tan, white, brown hair. Shorter, finer, and straighter than kitty cat Annie's, the fur was packed wad-tight. There wasn't much else. Well, something chestnut brown that could have been the outside of a seed. In the second turd, I found a treat, something I could recognize. The wing of a grasshopper. In my mind I heard fox teeth crunch through insect exoskeleton.

Waves crashing in my ears, salty scent in my nose, scat in my hand, I felt giddy. I was getting to know this fox! I snapped a selfie. What more could I want?

Answers.

Was that a seed? Do foxes eat grasshoppers often? Who do all these hairs belong to? How does Kat turn all her questions into answers? And what does this have to do with that question: "Do foxes belong on Fire Island?"

---

[7] The mitochondria is the powerhouse of the cell; it converts sugar into useful energy. The DNA in your cells' mitochondria is inherited from your mother. The DNA in your cells' nuclei is inherited from both parents.

I was dying to be in Kat's lab. How would she poop-sleuth?

Here's how she explained it: "We've got to split it up into the poop part—the unidentifiable digested waste material, aka, the crap—we don't need that. And then we have the prey remains like bones, hair, little chunks of shell." She held up labeled manila envelopes. If you've ever dissected an owl pellet, it's like that, only foxified.

"For some things, like a feather, it is really disintegrated, and we can't tell what kind it is, but some things like skulls are the Holy Grail."

Animals have unique skull shapes, eye sizes, and arrangements of teeth.[8] When you find a skull, you can whip out a dichotomous key and you are all set.[9] A dichotomous key is a numbered list that gives you choices like:

1a) Large skull over 75 mm long, go to step 2.
1b) Small skull under 75 mm long, go to step 6.

Following the steps, you might discover you're holding the skull of a flying squirrel in your hand!

But what about fur? A bunny, a deer, a squirrel—they are all brown. Kat let me in on her secret: microscope magic.

"So, on the outside, you've got cuticular scale patterns."

Cuti-what's? I didn't have a scope out there on Fire Island, but back at home I pulled some hairs from my ponytail holder and plopped them under my microscope. The outer layer, called the

---

[8] Kangaroo rats have inflated ear bones, so their skulls look triangular. House mice have a notch at the tip of their front teeth; harvest mice don't.

[9] When you find 433 samples of what could be fossilized feces, how do you sort them out? One bright student created a dichotomous key!

cuticle, was covered with small scales. On humans they don't look like fish scales, but on deer and on parts of Annie's fur they do. What about a river otter? Bunny? Opossum? In minutes my table was covered with strands plucked from every fur I could find.[10] Some scales looked like prim and proper hexagonal tiles, others like a 2-year-old's scribbling, still others reminded me of crowns stacked one on top of the other.[11]

The underfur of the river otter was completely different from his guard hairs. The guard hairs lay on the slide, chestnut brown, smoothly tapered at both ends, and standoffish from one another. With the underfur, I had to wrestle to get one strand wrenched away from the rest. I spun the dial and my scope zoomed in. It was wavy. Zoom, I spun again, going deeper and deeper into that world. It glistened. Zoom. Something, like tiny twists or diamond bits, winked out at me.

Thunk. That was my microscope hitting rock bottom. Oops. No more zoom for me.

But . . . but what was that winking?

Google Scholar to the rescue! Using an electron microscope, a scientist had photographed an otter's underfur. Along each segment of hair, 4 scales stick out like fins of a rocket. Each set of 4 is offset from the ones in the next segment, creating a jagged surface. Ah-ha! That's why I had trouble teasing the hairs apart. The scales of one hair grab onto the scales from another hair, causing them to interlock. That keeps water out and air bubbles in.[12] Next

---

[10] Don't worry. I took Annie's and Piper's from their combs.

[11] Did you know you can download "A Guide to the Identification of Irish Mammal Hair"? For free!? Plus, the FBI has an entire webpage devoted to the microscopic identification of animal hair.

[12] River otters don't have blubber like whales do. They count on their underfur to hold pockets of warm air against their skin, just like a puffy coat.

time I'm peering down at some scat and the hair winks up at me, I'll know exactly who has been eaten.

Suddenly, I'm gazing into a universe where hair matters. Instead of a brown squiggly thing, each hair is now an entire encyclopedia. My scope is my new best friend. I can't wait to order a new lens and get even more microscopic superpowers! Thank you, Kat!

What was the weirdest thing Kat found in scat? It didn't have cuticular scales, but a microscope had revealed the telltale clue: a wick. A fox had swallowed a strawberry-lemon scented candle. The fragrance was so strong that Kat could smell it through her face mask.

A fox eating a candle. That was just not right. I felt a waxy lump churn in my stomach.

Sadly, Kat's "Hall of Fame" included quite a few "not right" items: gum wrappers, bubble gum, neon pink turds.[13] It's pretty obvious: 4-legged friends have been playing in 2-legged trash. Kat had also found all the normal things and some island souvenirs—crabs and eggshells.

Scat is giving Kat all kinds of data to answer the "What do foxes on a barrier island eat?" question. But how about that other question? The "Do they belong?" question.

When an animal jumps off the mainland and onto an island, it is bound to mean something to the other island critters. In particular, people are wondering what it means to birds like piping plovers. A bird that is threatened. A bird that nests right on the ground.

A piping plover looks like a pencil sketch—stock-still and sky gray, with stark white and black trimmings tossed in for contrast.

---

[13] Once, I found green, rubbery goo in a pile of seaweed. Thinking it was one of those bouncy balls, I'd tossed it back and forth between my hands. Now I wonder, did it have its own tour of a digestive tract?

Each spring, plovers fly from winter homes (as far away as the Bahamas) to make summer homes on Fire Island. Mom and Pop Plover are cautious, taking up to 10 days to choose the best patch of sand for their nest. They scrape it clean, decorate it with shells, and produce pebble-sized eggs. The nest is so simple, the eggs so camouflaged, you could step on it if you aren't watching—or even if you are.

Only about 8,400 piping plovers are left on our planet. Why are they disappearing? People don't always spot the eggs in time to swerve. Plovers have definitely lost habitat to beach-side buildings—Mom and Pop Plover aren't okay with anything but prime real estate for their chicks. With water levels rising and people building barricades to keep storm tides back, smooth sandy washes are vanishing fast.

And then there are the predators. A piping plover chick may look like a puff of fluff, but on top of those pencil-yellow legs is a nice chomp of protein.

Are foxes eating the chicks? The eggs? The moms? The pops?

If they are, should we be doing something about it?

As Kat explained this, it sunk in just what her data might mean. At first my heart went out to the foxes. Then my heart went out to the plovers. Which is more important? I was torn between fluffy orange tails and fluffy peep-peeps!

Then my brain took over and said those decisions should be made with the head, not the heart.

Of course, the land managers on Fire Island were way ahead of me with all that. They knew they needed information to make good decisions.

How will they know if foxes are impacting the plover population?

Scat.

How will they know who else is involved?

Scat.

How will they know they've got solid data?

Scat.

Thank goodness for scat.

Thank goodness for Kat.

Kat's found bird remains (feathers, beak, bones) in 1 of every 4 scats, but they make up less than 10 percent of the total prey remains. Which bird species do they belong to?[14] Whose scats are those? Kat's still sleuthing through that. She's only 2.5 years into a 5-year study, so she doesn't have all the answers yet, but Kat's answers will matter.

---

[14] Once she did find a set of leg tags (like scientists put on birds) in a scat, so that one was pretty obvious. Typically, bird feathers get chewed up during digestion, making them hard to ID.

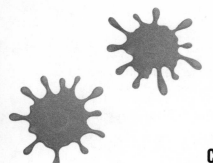

CHAPTER 11
FECAL FLOATS

One January afternoon, Piper and I were out exploring a steep-sided slope in the woods of Tennessee. The forest was dotted with limestone ledges, sinkholes, and stretches of streams that blinked out as they disappeared underground.[1] A great grand-daddy oak called out to me. Toppled by a storm, it leaned across the forest at a 35° angle.

I'd always wanted to explore tree canopies. That fallen oak was my easy button.

Up, up, up I scooched along the scratchy trunk. When I was 10 feet off the ground, my hand landed smack dab in the middle of a discovery. It wasn't a new plant or animal species; it was a pile of feces.[2] Actually it was more than one: dump after dump after dump lined up on the trunk. Someone had turned this tree into a toilet. Who? Why was there so much? And why bother

---

[1] This forest is located in TAG (Tennessee, Alabama, Georgia), a region famous for 14,000 caves. There, water drips, drips, drips, eating through limestone and leaving creepy cool crevices. We call them sinkholes or caves. Animals call them home.

[2] A new species of fly was discovered in duck droppings in Central Park, right in the middle of New York City! Apparently, the fly's larvae will eat only duck doo-doo—talk about a picky eater.

climbing up (or down) to go in this one spot?

Later, back in my office, I found a clue. There in the middle of a scientific paper, I read "raccoon latrines." Bingo! A phone call to Dr. Kristen Page, the author of that paper, confirmed the perpetrator: "Raccoons like to leave their piles of poo on elevated surfaces."[3] And for some reason, they keep coming back to the same spot. Why? After studying raccoon latrines for 25 years, even she doesn't have an answer. Most likely, it gives them a way to communicate.

That might have been the end of the story, except for one thing: Dr. Page studies the transmission dynamics of a parasite. What does that mean? And which parasite? And, when my hand landed in that latrine, did I catch the parasite?

I *needed* to know.

Formally, Dr. Kristen Page is a professor in the Biology Department at Wheaton College, where she holds the Ruth Kraft Strohschein Distinguished Chair. But as soon as she invited me to "sling some poop" in her lab, I knew that formal wasn't her style.

---

[3] In downtown Toronto, a coon climbed up a construction crane—700 feet up—to take a dump. There's a throne with a view!

From: Heather Montgomery
Date: Monday, April 16, 2018 at 1:20 PM
To: Kristen Page
Subject: Re: Information on raccoon roundworm

Do you know how happy it makes me to hear that your
students will be showing me fecal floats? ☺
Heather

From: Kristen Page
Sent: Monday, April 16, 2018 1:23 PM
To: Heather Montgomery
Subject: Re: Information on raccoon roundworm

We can go out for root beer floats afterward!
Kristen

Giggling and Googling, I found a plane ticket to Chicago.
A week later, I was standing in a small hall with locked doors at
both ends. Like at the airport checkpoint, Kristen asked me to take
off my shoes. Then she had me slip my feet into a pair of lab shoes,
Crocs that aren't ever allowed to leave the lab.[4] Unlike the airport
security system, which is designed to keep the bad guys *out*, this
system keeps bad guys *in*. Next, I had to put on gloves and then
tug another pair of gloves on top of those. We were entering a
place full of parasites!

When I stepped into Kristen's Disease Ecology Lab, the team
was ready. Rachel wore sporty neon shoes covered with confetti as

---

[4] To a microbe, is a shoe commute like a trip in a taxi or like the lift of a pole vault?

colorful as her enthusiasm. Nathan was tall and lanky, someone I'd want on my Ultimate Frisbee team. Rachel and Nathan are student volunteers digging in to make a difference. Their mission that morning? To find eggs of *Baylisascaris procyonis*,[5] the raccoon roundworm (RRW).

The lab room was flanked by two benches. Not benches you sit on—scientific benches, which look like metal countertops. They were loaded down with glass flasks, microscopes standing at attention, space-agey machines, and other nerdy science stuff.

The far end of one bench was covered in aluminum foil, like my mother's kitchen counter at candy-making time. Sitting on the foil were 20 or so plastic baggies, zipped up tight, each filled with a different shade of brown . . . No, not chocolate! A sweet collection of raccoon poo.

Each bag was labeled with a number, date, latitude, and longitude. Someone's GPS had been busy.

Finding the roundworm eggs in the poo is like an Easter egg hunt. Sounds fun except for one teeny-tiny fact: the eggs are teeny-tiny. Sure, you could saddle up on a laboratory stool and put a microscope to work, but think of all the mess you'd have to dig through. Rachel and Nathan put their science smarts to work instead.

Dense things sink.[6] For an example, just look in the loo—some days you find sinkers (more dense); some days you find floaters

---

[5] Raccoons are *Procyon lotor*—see the connection? The word *raccoon* comes from the Algonquin *arahkoonem* = they rub, scrub, scratch. Other names include the Delaware Indian *wtakalinch* = very clever with its fingers, and the Aztec *eeyahmahtohn* = little old lady who knows things.

[6] Density is a measure of how tightly matter is packed. $D = M/V$, how much mass there is per volume.

(less dense). *Baylisascaris* eggs aren't very dense, so if Rachel and Nathan can make everything else in the mix more dense, the eggs will rise to the top.

The key to their plan is simple: sugar.

Rachel smashed each scat sample and put a few crumbles or dribbles[7] into a Dixie cup. Nathan prepared a supersaturated sugar solution. Ever wanted to add more sugar to your drink but it just wouldn't dissolve? The liquid was saturated. To make it work, supersaturate it by heating it up. Chemistry at work. Yum-yum!

Next, they poured Nathan's super sweet goop into each Dixie cup. The dark crumbles swirled up to the top of the syrup. Maybe this is a fecal float?

With a Popsicle stick, Rachel stirred and stirred till she got diarrhea. Well, actually, it was the mixture that looked like diarrhea.

Then each sweet, stirred sample got its own little test tube and went for a spin in a centrifuge machine. The tubes sat in a circle like kids on that spinny carnival ride, but the slots in this machine leaned inward. When the tubes are spun, the densest stuff in the goop heads outward, toward the bottom of the tube.[8] And those eggs, they should rise to the top.

For 10 minutes the machine sounded like a tornado. When it was through, we had our fingers crossed. With an eye dropper–like pipette, the students slurped the top layer from each tube. The

---

[7] Humans use the Bristol Stool Chart (Type 1 = Hard lumps like peanuts; Type 7 = Entirely liquid) to compare poop consistencies. I wonder if coons ever do a compare/contrast.

[8] It's using centrifugal force, right? Not really. It's actually *centripetal* force. According to good ol' Isaac Newton, whenever a body is put into motion, it will continue in that direction. But the tubes aren't moving in a straight line; they are curving. The walls of the machine are applying a force perpendicular to their forward motion. It's like the wall of a car pushing you around a bend in the road. That force is *centripetal* force. Ask a physics teacher and they'll tell you centrifugal force is only an *apparent* force. It's all about perspective!

rest of the glop got slopped into a "poop bucket." You wouldn't want to trip on that.

Drip-drop, they plopped sample after sample on slides. Later, Kristen would slip the slides under a scope to see if any of those coon scats were infected with the eggs of squirmy worms. Why are these little worm eggs such a big deal? Dr. Page is on a mission to save thousands of lives. But it's not the little masked bandits she's worried about.

You see, RRWs don't mind their own business. They don't keep to the coons. They require a second host to complete their life cycle, and that's why those wormies are causing all kinds of a ruckus.

RRWs are curvy and tan or white and look like overgrown bean sprouts. The adults hang out in the small intestines of—surprise, surprise—raccoons. In one spot, 82 percent of coons were infested. An average worm burden is 50 worms. A female worm can be longer than a pencil.[9] That's a lot of squirmy in anybody's tummy, but worms in coon tummies aren't the *real* burden.

Each mama worm pumps out ~100,000 eggs a day. A day! That's 20,000 eggs in every gram of coon scat. Just think of how many might be incubating in one raccoon latrine. Every trip to the toilet, a raccoon could unknowingly pick up more eggs on her paws, then add more eggs to her breakfast. But even that's not the real burden. The worms aren't a coon's BFF, but for the most part, they just cycle through their ring-tailed hosts.

The *real* burden comes if you are a bird or a small mammal

---

[9] The guys are half as long.

and you swallow the eggs. Kittens, kingbirds, kinkajous?[10] Yep, these wormies have a special place in their hearts for furred and feathered friends.[11] Inside a warm mammal or bird belly, the larva bursts out. This is no cute caterpillar. The larva pierces the gut wall and invades his host's body. He's looking for a place to pause till he can complete his life cycle. In many cases, he'll encyst into a nice tight ball. A place he can wait and wait and wait, hoping his host will get gobbled by a coon. *If* that happens, I guess it's like winning the lottery. Inside the coon, the lucky larva will get to grow up to be a mama or papa worm.

But who wants to leave it to chance? Instead of encysting, some larvae insist on hitchhiking to the brain. There, their superparasitic powers kick in.

One of their pivotal powers? Inflaming a brain. And just what does a little mammal with a bulging brain do? Oh, it walks in circles, chasing its tail. Or it stands, back arched, head up, stock-still as if stargazing in the middle of the day. Neither strategy is any good for avoiding death.

And guess who might decide that that dead body is as easy as takeout?

Yep. Raccoons are omnivores.

✔ Corn
✔ Crayfish
✔ Carrion

---

[10] A kinkajou looks like a Virginia opossum with a buzz cut. It's the color of honey, has a grab-the-branch tail, a pink button nose, and feet that can flip forward or backward. I thought kinkajous were primates, but they are actually raccoon relatives who live in Central and South America.

[11] That's a lie. RRWs are so small and simple, they don't need a circulatory system. They're heartless.

It's all on their menu.[12] So, that's how RRWs are causing a ruckus. When little larvae tunnel in, they take over more than masked bandits.

In Kristen's lab, I also got a good look at coon guts. Two other students, Tim and Laura, performed necropsies[13] just for me!

"I'm always astonished by just how cool the mesentery is," Tim marveled as he leaned over a white, lasagna-sized pan. Draped across his left hand was the end of a flattened pink tube. In his right hand, scissors.

"Just look at that." He held up a section of pink intestine webbed together by a film as clear as cellophane. Bloodred vessels stream through the film, headed toward a liver. "A work of art!"

It was as intricate as a stained glass window.

Tim's fingers cradled the segment of raccoon gut. Clip-slip, clip-slip, he clipped vessels then slipped the blade through the clear mesentery. He stood on my left, Laura, on my right. Each had the entire digestive tract from one raccoon, from mouth to, well, the other end. As they snipped, they compared the contents. Kristen roamed behind us, ready to do anything that required "clean" hands. Above the intestines, the conversation flitted around:

"There's a lot of stool."

"Oozing out."

"This one doesn't look like it's had a meal in a while."

"It's starving!"

"There's some hair."

---

[12] Not that scrubbing would get rid of the worms, but FYI, raccoons don't "wash" their food. When coons dunk food, the water fires up nerve cells in their skin. If your eyesight wasn't so strong, you'd be a fan of fingers that can feel exactly what you were about to put on your tongue.

[13] Necropsy: a surgical exam of a dead body—like an autopsy but with a nonhuman subject. How many gross -opsy words are there?

"Pink speckles."

"Sometimes you see tails of mice."

And just when their gloves were good and goopy: "Your nose always itches in the middle of a necropsy."

With a small metal spatula, Laura scooped out stool from deep in a colon. She smeared it into a vial Kristen was holding. "It's so gloopy. I'm sorry." Laura worked the lip of the vial, trying to wrangle the brown back in. That vial was headed to Dr. Holly Lutz at the Field Museum, who was eager to sequence the DNA from a coon's microbiome.

Tim frowned. Laura grimaced. They weren't here to show me what raccoons eat. They weren't even here to scoop stool for Holly Lutz—that was a bonus. Bacteria aren't the bad guys they were after. They weren't even looking for RRW Easter eggs. No, this team had something a little more ropey in mind. They were on the hunt for adult worms.

Thirty minutes later, the guts lay splayed open from one end to the other, contents stirred and searched. Tim and Laura, necks stiff, gloves painted with brown, gave up. Not a single RRW in either specimen.

This *should* be a good thing. Why are the students so disappointed?

Kristen aims to put a damper on the RRW population of Chicago. She's kind of a pro at tracking down infested coon populations and knocking out their populations of worms. But to do this, she needs to know where the infestations are. That's why she had guts collected from neighborhoods across the Windy City.[14]

---

[14] Chicago seems to be a hotspot for RRWs. No one knows why. Maybe the worms like the weather!

These necropsies with no worms meant she'd have to keep looking.

Finding the worms is only the first step. Nestled in soil, RRW eggs can last 10 years. How do you get rid of millions of micro-scopic eggs? Are *you* going to volunteer to pick them up one by one by one?

Make sure you wash your hands.

Oh, wait, soap doesn't kill them. That chemical that biology labs smell like—formalin—it doesn't kill them either. Bleach? It removes their protein coat, leaving them slimy enough to slip-slide away. Goodie-goodie.

To kill them in the soil, you could use a blowtorch.

1) Purchase a Red Dragon Vapor Torch.
2) Fire it up.
3) Blast away till the soil is red- to white-hot.
4) Move to the next spot.

Are you really going to do that for all of Chicagoland? Where do you even start? A suburban park? Dumpsters downtown? What if you start a fire?[15]

Thank goodness Kristen has a better solution: the necropsies tell her where the wormies are hanging out, and then she can put medicated marshmallows to work. Dewormers go right down the gullet when tucked inside those sweet spongy treats.

---

[15] You know that camp song "Old Lady Leary"? It's about how a cow kicked over a lantern and started the Great Chicago Fire of 1871. A fire so hot it even burned the river! Yep, oily pollution floating on top of a river can burn.

Part of this story is all about rats. I know, I know, who loves a rat, right? I'll admit, when Kristen first said that three-letter word—a word that conjures up dirty, greasy, trash-eating varmints—I wasn't jumping for joy. Usually I root for the underdogs, but a rat?[16]

Yes, a rat. In fact, that rat had me jet-setting all the way to New York City. The next day, I was up before dawn, my field bag packed, and headed into the woods with Gretchen Fowles of the New Jersey Division of Fish & Wildlife and her crew of volunteers. We weren't after the sewer-scurrying Norway rat.[17] We were on the hunt for the endangered Allegheny woodrat. Pair the word *endangered* with any species name, and you've got my attention.

Back in the day, Allegheny woodrats lived as far north as Connecticut and all the way down the line of mountains through Tennessee and into the northern part of Alabama. But by 2004, they were on more state endangered species lists than any other rodent. No one is sure what's doing them in, but ideas include everything from deforestation to human disturbance to climate change to the blight that knocked out the American chestnut.[18] Or maybe it's raccoon roundworms.

Allegheny woodrats like it dark. They live in caves or on limestone-covered slopes where their nests can be tucked into secret crevices for safety. When the sun sets, the rats scamper out to get the groceries. Their favorite foods? Fruits, fungi, nuts, and,

---

[16] Now, rat scat can do cool stuff. In one study, glow-in-the-dark rat turds helped fight obesity. Really! Want to know more? Check out the annotated bibliography at the end of the book.

[17] Norway rats are famous for a few things, notably spreading the PLAGUE! New research using mathematical models shows that maybe those rats were innocent all along.

[18] Oaks produce acorns in boom and bust years. That's all well and good for a quick reproducer like a white-footed mouse, who can pop out more babies in a boom year to make up for the bust years. Some scientists think slow-reproducing woodrats coevolved with steady nut-producers like the American chestnut—a tree that died off in the first half of the 1900s.

most importantly, seeds. Typically, the seeds are scattered, so a rat has to shop all across the forest to find them.

A night when a woodrat finds a raccoon latrine must feel like Halloween—a coon turd is a tidy tube bursting with bunches of savory seeds. The little squeaker hauls his booty home and stashes the turd in a midden, a heap that might also contain bones, toys from two-leggeds, and rat droppings. He pees on the pile. The urine crystalizes and holds it all together like glue.[19]

Little does he realize there's a secret ingredient inside those turds . . . now his pantry is fully stocked with invisible roundworm eggs. *Nom-nom-nom*, he gnaws into a few seeds and down his gullet those eggs go. It's time for them to start their own version of mind control. It's time for them to inflame his brain.

The threat of extinction is why this team of volunteers was willing to follow Gretchen, to high-step our way through a jungle of poison ivy, to risk our ankles and knees as gritty gray rocks shifted under our boots. We were about to knock on the door of the only Allegheny woodrat population in the entire state.

Just across the Hudson River, we could hear the trains, pile drivers, and traffic of the big city, but Palisades Park is a pocket of wild. An osprey screamed overhead. Copperheads lounged on the rocks.[20] Hairy, white fox scat crunched under our boot soles.

Up, up, up we scampered toward two stone slabs leaning together and marked with a spray-painted dot. Once a year in very

---

[19] If kept dry, a midden can last a l-o-o-n-g time. To scientists, they are treasure troves of info. Sifting through plant bits from an ancient midden, someone figured out how plant populations shifted up and down the walls of the Grand Canyon as a result of climate change over 11,000 years ago.

[20] One year, one team member broke her leg—not from slip-sliding down that treacherous slope but because she tried to hop-skip over a copperhead.

111

specific spots, this team sets out live traps, baits them with apples and peanut butter, then crosses its fingers.

Were any woodrats lured in last night?

They let me—ME!—squirm into the slot to recover the trap. Feet up in the air, head buried under a rhino-sized rock, I teeter-tottered, almost sliding too far and plowing nose-first into a carpet of scat. Then, I turned my head and met my first woodrat.

It took exactly 0.001 of a second for me to fall in love. She had floppy Dumbo ears, button eyes, and whiskers way out to there. She was the color of a white potato but the shape of a sweet potato. Her little pink paw stretched out of the metal mesh and landed on my finger.

I touched an endangered species.

I *held* an endangered species!

My pinkie gave a high five to an Allegheny woodrat—a moment I'll never forget.

As her tiny toe pads pressed their pinkness into my skin, that sweet potato and I exchanged more than heat. My heart was trampolining up toward the moon; then my brain whispered something sinister.

Roundworms.

What if this sweet potato had been lured in by the scent of coon scat? What if little larvae were—right at this moment—migrating to her brain? What if she starts chasing her tail round and round out there, exposed on those wide-open spaces? There wouldn't be any merry on that go-round.

She would get chomped.

Maybe an eagle. Maybe a copperhead. Maybe a coon.

That vicious cycle could start all over again.

But that one little death wasn't enough buzzkill for my brain. No, it insisted, there's way more than that. Another woodrat will happen along. He's looking for new digs, and this sweet shelter is vacant. Bonus: the pantry is stocked. Turd tarts, poop pops, scat snacks. Sold! He moves in. He gnaws in. Too soon, his brain is bursting and then he's doing the circle-circle dance, too.

Like gritty gray rocks under my weight, something inside me shifted.

That spiteful cycle powered by poo might be wiping woodrats right off the map.

Back in Chicago in Kristen Page's office, my mind wasn't on raccoons or roundworms. I was ogling a tapeworm in a jar (biologists have the most intriguing knickknacks). Kristen was talking woodrats when she let it slip that she caught histoplasmosis from feces.

Histo—what? I dragged my eyes away from a skunk skull and placed them firmly on her face.

"It's a fungal infection and the fungus grows on scat and I was in caves. I got really sick, like pneumonia." She nodded. "I recovered from the lung infection but somehow the spores went to my reti-nas. So, when I get really stressed out, or eat the wrong things, the inflammation starts and I can't see out of my left eye."

"Wait—" I couldn't fathom something as scary as going blind, even if it only happens sometimes. "But you are still working with poop?" I sat back, trying to wrap my mind around that kind of ded-ication. "Is it worth it?"

"Mmm-hmmm." Kristen nodded again, and then suddenly her whole body went still.

"Children die from this parasite."

Oh. In all that fascination with an endangered species, I had kind of skipped over the fact that people are mammals. People can become infected, too.

My mouth went dry.

Most often the people who get roundworms are the ones who eat dirt.

Who eats dirt?

Kids. Because they explore everything with their hands and mouths, little kids eat it all the time. When toddlers see something interesting, they pop it into their mouth. What looks like a pile of innocent berries—yum-yum—might be berries that have gone through a coon tum-tum.

According to one report, there were 14 cases of humans infected by raccoon roundworms over a span of 30 years. But many doctors don't know about RRWs, so it can easily go undiagnosed. Who knows how many cases have been missed?[21] And we are talking

---

[21] On a TV show called *House*, medical detectives spent a whole episode misdiagnosing a fictionalized version of these little buggers. The truth is even scarier than that fiction.

about toddlers here. When a toddler's wailing, how are you supposed to know something sad is going on inside his skull?[22] [23]

We weren't joking about floats anymore.

"We usually do not figure out that they are sick until they have devastating brain injury that is *not* reversible. One of the very first cases was a little boy named Tommy, and he was maybe 18 months old.

"And he got really sick and essentially it progressed till he was blind and deaf ...

"and he didn't speak again ...

"and he didn't walk again."

Tommy was a fighter. He made it to 18 years old before he died.

My questions have taken a deep dark turn. Raccoon latrines are no longer fun and fascinating. The idea that feces are full of bad stuff is no longer a nagging thought in the back of my brain. No longer words on a page. No longer someone else's problem. It is a rock crushing my gut.

It had been raining for days, cold rain for days and days, and then it stopped. Piper and I set out to find an adventure. We were roaming the Tennessee woods collecting tiny treasures: bright purple seeds, antler-shaped lichen, an odd green growth from a tree. A new spring ran from one of the limestone outcroppings. Limestone

---

[22]For some unknown reason, almost every known case has been in boys.

[23]Out in California, a little boy got sick. The hospital sent him home, saying it was a virus. The next day he wasn't nursing right, so his mom took him back. They sent him home again. The third day, his mom was sure he couldn't see, so she took him back. Inside his eye? One roundworm larva.

outcroppings that I now knew may once have housed Allegheny woodrats. Following the water down from the spring, we suddenly found ourselves near that very same storm-toppled oak—the one that started this whole raccoon roundworm journey.

Gravity had pulled the oak closer to the ground. I hesitated, then ventured along its flattened, flaking trunk. At the spot where the coon poop had been piled, all was washed away.[24] On a branch that angled below the main trunk, a small hollow cupped two turds.

A Carolina wren *scrrrrt-scrrrted*, warning me away. Coon turds had led me to this story I needed to scrub from my mind.

The wren's right. There is nothing good here.

As I pushed home, past a scurrying salamander, the opening to a sinkhole, a pile of deer droppings, not a single question called out to me.

There were no tears, no angry words.

Nothing.

My curiosity had run cold.

---

[24] I know better than that. One kid got RRW from playing with clean-looking firewood. Microscopic eggs lurk on logs.

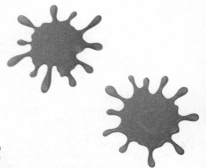

CHAPTER 12
PANDAS, POETRY, AND PALM OIL

I was sick and tired of poop. I did not want to talk about it, hear about it, read about it.

Poop emojis popped up on my phone. Poop dolls danced in store windows. Ads for a poop café flashed in my feed.[1] Everywhere I turned: poop, Poop, POOP!

Poop was trending, and with every single sighting, my mind turned to: bad, bad, bad.

I had an interview scheduled with another researcher, Dave Hemprich-Bennett. Cancel it—that was my plan. But Dave's poop study was about a place I had been worrying about, the rainforests of Asia. In those lands lush with limbs, green granddaddy trees are being hacked to the ground to make way for palm plantations. Row upon row of the exact same tree—where's the biodiversity in that?

Palm plantations are all about oil. Not the black stuff from underground—the red stuff from palm tree fruit and the pee-colored

---

[1] Cute poop cafés in Canada and Korea offer toilet-shaped seats, turdy ice cream in potty-shaped bowls, and blue poo hats as souvenirs. Korea has a poo museum where you can learn how people used rope for toilet paper. In Japan, turd-themed textbooks are legendary.

stuff squeezed from palm tree seeds. Palm oil is in everything these days: cookies, cake, candy, crackers, creamer, chips, chocolate, and canned soup, and that's just in the kitchen. In the bathroom, there's shampoo, shaving cream, soap, sunscreen. "S-S-S-S-S-S-Stop chopping our trees-s-s-s," the snakes have to be hissing. People say palm oil's in 50 percent of the products on grocery-store shelves. It hides behind aliases, like *vegetable oil, palmate, sodium laureth sulfate,* Elaeis guineensis, and *stearic acid.*[2] It's EVERYWHERE!

---

[2] I'm sure I missed a few. There's, like, 200 alter egos for palm oil.

Why is palm oil such a "thing"? For one thing, it's fat (yum-yum) that doesn't contain trans fat—the stuff in doughnuts, fried food, and commercially processed baked goods that bumps up the chance you'll keel over from a heart attack. For another thing, it's cheap. When folks got all uptight about trans fat, food companies said swip-swap, palm oil will work just fine for those fries.

Palm oil plantations have spread like a rash: Africa, Borneo, Central America, Malaysia . . . Row upon row of tidy ferny fronds now stand where a jumbly jungle of vines, shrubs, and trees should be. Palm oil crops cover an estimated 61 million acres. That's more land than the entire United Kingdom!

Ask the Palm Oil Awareness Initiative, and they'll tell you a few animals who are paying the price for our palm oil propensities:

One) Orangutans

Two) Tigers

Three) Tapirs

Four) Fishing cats

Five) Flat-headed cats

Six) Sumatran rhinoceroses

Seven) Sunda clouded leopards

Eight) Elephants

Nine) I have to stop because I don't think I can swallow. All those animals; all that lost habitat. If you add in insects, it feels like the list could go on to infinity.[3]

---

[3] Concerned scientists say the number of total species in danger is closer to 193, but what about all those species we don't yet know about?

Bottom line? Palm oil is Enemy #1 in animal lovers' eyes. A few weeks earlier, I had read a book about orangutans and how their playgrounds were being wiped out by the demand for palm oil. I raided my pantry, ready to cross every offending item off my grocery list.

Consequently, I had been looking forward to talking with Dave. A researcher at the University of Oxford, he was using bat guano from Malaysia to piece together the ecology of those rainforests. I *couldn't* cancel the interview. I needed to know just how nasty palm oil was.

So, I cranked up the computer, clicked on Skype, and dove into one more poopy conversation. Dave isn't afraid to dedicate his life, his brains, even his body to save animal lives. During his college years, he got to pick through caiman puke for the good of science. Now, he's turned to the other end of the tube. Traipsing through the rainforest to get guano, he gained a few rainforest friends. Hookworm friends. Friends who lodged themselves in his ... um ... Dave's British, so let's just say "bum."

His work is complex. You remember what my bat guano looked like? All the insects mushed together in a hodgepodge of parts? Now think about how many more insects live in the rainforest. To see what his bat buddies were eating, Dave turned technical and dove into the DNA. When we talked, he was in the middle of matching up all those A's, T's, C's, and G's.

His bigger goal, however, is to understand the ecological network of the rainforest. An ecological network is a model of how all the living things in an entire system connect. All the living things. Type "ecological network" into an internet search, and you'll see colors and lines shooting everywhere—left, right, across, up, down, even around. This is no simple *x, y* plot. No tidy textbook diagram of a food chain. Put that on steroids.

The guano gives Dave the data he needs, but the system's so complex, we need to think of it in 3D. Thank goodness for computers. Call each critter a "node" and give it a color code. Then start connecting the dots. And pretty soon, out cranks a chart that looks like spaghetti. There are so many lines, you can't tell who's connected to who.[4]

I'm sitting back, smiling and nodding, because I just know what this is going to prove—that every single species matters a whole awful lot, and we should never ever set saw to a single rainforest tree.

And *then* Dave suggests that maybe palm plantations aren't Enemy #1.

Wait . . . What?!

"If, as a world of 7 billion people, we need to feed everyone"—his nose ring bobbed as that problem contorted his face—"we need some sort of vegetable oil for it."

Palms, he explains, are actually more productive than other crops.

"If you were to use soy to generate the same amount of oil, you'd need 8 times as much land converted from rainforest to soy."

Imagine 8 times the forest hacked!

Oh.

"Yeah, this is having a negative effect on this area, but if it were to be soy, it would be Brazil's Atlantic rainforest."

---

[4] Just like in the lunchroom or any social media platform, certain nodes show up as the strongest influencers. So much traffic headed their way, the individual lines blur into one dark mass.

The awesome orangutans of Asia or the hootin' howler monkeys of Brazil—which animals are the right ones to save? My mind flashes back to the red foxes and the piping plovers.

"So," Dave continues, "we are seeing this forest being chopped down to grow this. And that is very powerful and difficult. A lot of conservationists or environmentalists tend to just say a blanket statement: We should boycott palm oil." Dave proposes that there needs to be compromise.

"It's not black and white."

He hopes his results will help people make the best decisions about which areas to cut and which to protect. There is no simple answer from a simple pile of poo.

When I get off the call, my mind is spinning like a cartoon character who's been bopped in the head. Boycotting palm oil had seemed like the right thing to do. But now . . .

By switching from my favorite cereal to a palm oil–free brand, had I committed more acres to the ax, just in a different place? What was I supposed to do?

For one thing, I wasn't going to just take his opinion about it. I knew where I could find some answers. Pretty soon I was eyeball-deep in scientific studies, megabytes deep in videos, and eardrums-deep in podcasts. Everyone had an opinion, but Dave wasn't alone with his ideas. The UCS, IUCN, WWF[5]—all the letters of the environmental movement came to the same conclusion: a boycott is not the answer.

Then, what is!?

---

[5] UCS = Union of Concerned Scientists; IUCN = International Union for Conservation of Nature; WWF = World Wildlife Fund.

As all this was bashing on my brain, something else hit me hard. I was chatting with Dr. Ashli Brown at Mississippi State about her panda poo project.

A panda gut does something phenomenal—it turns bamboo into energy. Have you tried to break bamboo? Crazy tough stuff. How do pandas work their magic? Microbes, of course.[6] Ashli and her team wondered, if you steal microbes from panda stool and feed those microbes waste wood, could they pump out biofuel?

She explained how pandas are oddballs: "They are carnivorous herbivores—an oxymoron really."[7] Their ancestors were carnivores; now all they eat is bamboo. The switch from one diet to the other took place 2 million or so years ago; yet, their guts still don't look like other herbivores' guts. "They lack the digestive adaptations you typically see. They don't have a long cecum; they're not hind-gut fermenters; and they aren't ruminants like cows.

"Evolutionarily the panda bear is pretty unique," Ashli says, then pauses. "And then there is the opposite end of the coin, where people say, 'Maybe they are endangered for a reason.'"

Huh? I clamped my tongue between my teeth so that I wouldn't interrupt her explanation.

"Maybe, you know, it's not the best system. Maybe they have run their course."

It sounded as if she were proposing that pandas *should* be extinct. Right away, though, she clarified her opinion: we should

---

[6] Some of those microbes are cousins to *C. diff*! One study found that if you stir panda poo into 24 kg of kitchen waste, the microbes reduce it to 1 kg in just one month. Major garbage guzzling!

[7] No, she's not saying pandas are morons! An oxymoron is a combination of words that seem contradictory.

be saving the panda because humans are playing a huge role in their decline. But for weeks after our chat, the thought that a species *should* go extinct haunted my heart.

Now, my brain knew that extinction is normal. When a creature's adaptations don't match up to the environmental conditions it likes, it's bye-bye brontosaurus. An estimated 99.9 percent of the species that have ever graced this planet have gone extinct.

That's right: 99.9 percent.

Just because I knew it didn't mean I wanted to believe it.

Sure, I can swallow the extinction of all those ancient beasts, back when nature was taking its course. But now, when people are messing things up?

A little voice whispered in the back of my brain: If humans never had any impact, would pandas naturally go extinct? What about clouded leopards? Or those Dumbo-eared cuties, the Allegheny woodrats?

How are we supposed to know?

Science is supposed to be giving me answers. Supposed to help me know what to do. Every single day I make choices I think are helping endangered species. Recycling, buying organic, nixing my favorite cereal from my grocery list. What if those choices are not *the* answer?

I do not know what to do with this information.

My head hurts.

This knot is tangled tighter than otter intestines.

It was 3:21 a.m. when I gave up and dragged myself out of bed. My brain was roiling with unanswered questions. There was no way it was going to let me get any Z's.

Hoping for peace, I pulled out a book about poetry. From the top of the page, a quote shouted at me:

The question is not what you look at,
but what you see.
–Henry David Thoreau

My mind scrolled back to the day I had puzzled through a hodgepodge of insect parts. The day that yellow knob, filled with windows and prisms, caught my attention. The day I had tried to put poop together like a photo on a jigsaw puzzle box.

Sitting there with the darkness trying to swallow me whole, I knew there was so much more to poop than a pretty picture.

What if all this time I had been seeing the wrong thing? Focused on the bits and pieces, had I let unanswered edges slice away at my attention?

Maybe if I stepped back, I would see it more like a collage, a piece of poetry, a stained glass window.

What if each scat is just one little piece of a larger idea? What if each study could shine new light on that idea? What if the "right" answer is to keep stick-stirring through tough questions, to pick up that insect eye, and to willingly see the world through a new lens?

CHAPTER 13
POOP AND PREJUDICE

"Hey, Heather, guess what I have in my backyard?" When my friend Cynthia calls, you never know what is coming next.

"Dead or alive?" I asked.

"Dead."

It was December 24, and I should have been wrapping gifts. Forget that! I hotfooted it over a few hills and down into a holler where Cynthia gifted me with a dead possum. At her bluegrass holiday party a week or so before, I had whined about needing an omnivore. I had poked through the contents of carnivore stomachs; I had wound my way through herbivore intestines; but I had not yet traveled an awesome omnivore gut.

When you need a dead body, you can always count on friends (and a hound dog named Beatrice).

The opossum's tail was a scaled marvel that made me think of a pangolin. I ran my finger along it and the pink tip gripped.[1] Was he playing dead?

---

[1] Great Gripper: A Virginia opossum uses her nearly hairless tail like a safety belt when climbing, for carrying twigs and leaves to her den, or as a kickstand when standing on 2 legs. Mom and Pop Possum can't hang by their tails for long, but young ones can.

Unfortunately not.[2]

A few hours later I was sitting happily at my dining room table with his digestive tract sprawled out in front of me. The faces of friends and family looked down at me from holiday cards standing on the other end of the table. What would my friends say if they could peek out through those eyes?

I worked my way up from the tail end. The first four inches of colon were empty, then there was a nickel-width lump. Snip-snip. The intestine was cotton-candy pink and lined with wrinkles where it wasn't full. The first turd sat dark and glossy, just larger than a jelly bean and covered in mucus.

Under the force of my probe, the turd split in half, the mucus stretching across the gap like tinsel over a doorway. One lumpy booger perched at the far end. I leaned in with my loupe, ready for treasure.

Something made me shudder.

I worked the probe through the turd. Dirt brown, with a mushroomy odor. Something hard and shaped like the tip of a tongue. Fine, cobwebby hairs. But my eyes kept straying back to that booger. I gave in and reached for it. It clung to my probe tip. As I lifted, it uncoiled like a string.

Something squirmed in my intestines.

Segment after segment spooled out from the bugger till my brain shouted, "TAPEWORM!"

The probe clattered. Piper jumped up. Annie mewed in surprise.

Can this parasite go airborne? Have I put Piper and Annie in danger?

---

[2] When a possum plays dead, he has no control over muscles like the anal sphincter, which means poop oozes out. Don't laugh, it could happen to you.

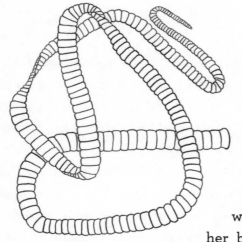

A single tapeworm can stretch almost a 100 feet long. A man pulled one right out of his rectum and wrapped it around a toilet paper roll to carry it to the emergency room. A nearly unconscious 8-year-old girl was carted into the hospital, her body racked with seizures. Approximately 100 white dots—tapeworm larvae—sat silently in her brain. Sounds suspiciously like the tale of the raccoon round-worm to me.[3]

Through my mask I took a deep breath and recited all my pre-cautions. Then I rationalized: Tapeworms are spread through ingestion. Not through the air. Piper's survived many a sniff-sniff of a dead animal, and there's no way I'm letting Annie lick my lab table. We *should* be safe.

The second turd contained two things that looked like teeth but seemed too large for possum prey's teeth. Claw tips? Did he bite his nails? Bird beaks? Do possums eat birds?

Farther up the large intestine, where things were soupy, I found a bulge filled with tube-shaped worms all swirled together. Ugh. They were thread-thick and less than a centimeter long. Dis-tinctly different from the tapeworm. What are they? I quit count-ing at 23. UGGHHH! I wanted to eradicate every parasite from this poor possum's body.

---

[3] How do we know the life cycle of pork tapeworms? In 1855, a mad scientist fed infected pork to condemned prisoners and then (after their death) dug into their brains!

Keep looking.

I swallowed hard to settle the bile in my throat and clipped 21 inches farther to the thumb-sized cecum.

The stench I could stomach. The brown ooze making its way across the tablecloth, I could deal with. But when white worms started clinging to my gloves, I wigged out, almost flinging the gloves across the room.

Keep going.

Clenching my teeth, I took it one snip-slip at a time. The journey took me past seeds the shape of bird heads, a 4-inch grass stem, and intestinal walls so thin they looked like white tights. Ahead was a bulge the width of a quarter and 3 inches long, the last before the white pear of a stomach.

Snip.

Not 1 or 2 or 20—or any countable number—but an entire stew of worms washed out. All those worms were helminths, a group of parasitic worms that plague the planet.[4] There was this guy, Jasper Lawrence, who took himself all the way to Africa to find a helminth.

He didn't want to see it. He didn't want to catch it in a container. He wanted to catch it in his body.

You've got to be kidding me.

The story was, he walked barefoot through human excrement to infect himself with hookworms. That story seemed so fake, I didn't even investigate.

Months later, though, as I scrolled through Erin McKenney's website, the word *helminth* jumped out and latched onto me. The word was sitting there, all innocent in the middle of a title, among words that drew me in closer and closer and closer.

---

[4] Raccoon roundworms are helminths.

Prevents

Immune

Dysfunction

There's a lot in the news about autoimmune diseases—things like inflammatory bowel disease (IBD)[5] and multiple sclerosis[6]—where people's immune systems are dysfunctional—they go haywire and attack their own bodies. Had Erin discovered a way to put the brakes on those kinds of diseases?

Click. Soon my screen was sprawling with science. The full title was, "Got Worms? Perinatal Exposure to Helminths Prevents Persistent Immune Sensitization and Cognitive Dysfunction Induced by Early-Life Infection."

That was more than a mouthful. I churned through the words for over an hour but still didn't get it.

The study was based on earlier research by Dr. William Parker, a guy who went dumpster diving for rats. He had compared the wild guts of dumpster rats to the clean guts of lab rats.[7] That led him to a hypothesis that helminths could affect the entire ecosystem in the gut.

Open wide, little rats! Time for your tapeworms.[8]

Dr. Parker had recruited Erin to peek into the rats' ceca. She compared the microbiome of rats with worms to rats without squirms.

---

[5] 1.4 million people in the US have IBD—hot red sores or painful lumpy bumps lining the inside of their bowel. Most of them live in the north. Why? Erin says it might be a lack of vitamin D.

[6] With MS, the immune system attacks the protective covering of its own nerves. No one knows the cause. No one knows the cure.

[7] Which guts would you want?

[8] Poor rats. Why are they always our guinea pigs? Blame it on their genes. For every human gene linked to a disease, a rat has a similar one. There are 30 Nobel Prize–winning studies—tuberculosis, typhus, tumors—all thanks to rat superstars. Did they get credit? Nope.

She found that 20 percent of the bacteria were a different species! Look out the window and imagine 1 in every 5 plants suddenly swapped out for something else. Astounding.

On top of that, this difference didn't seem to be a random change. The rats with happy helminths had more of the beneficial fiber-digesting bacteria than those clean-gutted rats.

Huh.

For hundreds of millions of years, animal bodies have had one-way guts. And you better believe worms found their way into those guts. Think of the tapeworm that could live in a *T. rex*![9] It's like animal innards have never known life without worms. Like they evolved together.

Scientists get all geeked out over that kind of coevolution. Erin had described it as a 3-legged stool.[10] You've got the animal tissue, the worm, and the microbes, all supporting each other down in that deep, dark intestine.

"When you remove the helminths," she said, "then you only have two legs on the stool and that is super wobbly."

Erin had me super curious about helminths so I hopped a plane, waded through a tropical storm, and waltzed into the office of Dr. Peter Hotez. Dr. Hotez is the head of the Texas Children's Center for Vaccine Development, is known worldwide as an expert on human health, and was selected as a science envoy to the president

---

[9] Eggs of several different helminths have been found in fossilized dino poop. None in *T. rex*, yet, so that discovery could be yours!

[10] *Stool* in the kitchen versus *stool* in the toilet. This lucky word is a homonym, which means it has two different meanings that are spelled and pronounced the same.

of the United States. Now, he is the dean of the National School of Tropical Medicine at Baylor College of Medicine.

Dr. Hotez has spent his career fighting the diseases of people living in poverty. At the top of his hit list: helminths. "There are 800 million people with Ascaris, the human roundworm, 400 plus each with hookworm and whipworm."

The idea of treating yourself with worms, he says, "is based on misinformation and erroneous understandings about parasites."

Helminths cause all kinds of problems: 1) Whipworms may be the leading cause of inflammatory bowel disease. 2) Roundworms can cause asthma.[11] 3) Human hookworm makes kids stupid.[12] Worms and similar diseases are as bad as heart disease and cancer *and* they have the ability to cause poverty.

One of Dr. Hotez's greatest accomplishments: the first worm vaccine in the world.

As I left his office, I walked down a hospital-like hallway surrounded by a swarm of scientists. I should have been comforted by the flapping of their official badges, the slapping of shoes on spick-and-span tile floor. Somehow, I wasn't.

I had come to Houston looking for answers; I left with one big question: are helminths good or bad?

Dr. William Parker studied rats, but the guts he really cares about belong to two-leggeds. Just minutes into our Skype conversation,

---

[11] Kids in Norway who have roundworms from dogs are 4 times as likely to get asthma and allergies. Oddly, the same isn't true for their parents. Why? Who knows.

[12] Hookworm larvae prick the skin of bare feet and inch their way inside. A 1926 study of kids in Alabama showed that the more hookworm they had, the lower their intelligence. Is that a correlation or a causation?

I can tell he's thrown his heart and soul into solving human suffering. He's not a doctor in the "medical doctor" sense of the term. In fact, his PhD is in biophysics, but he's done research about all-too-common human conditions: allergies, autism, multiple sclerosis. One of the most infuriating things about those conditions is that traditional medicine doesn't have a cure for them.

Dr. Parker has got ideas, and there's nothing traditional about them.

"Bottom line: we need to reconstitute our biome to get the worms back."

You read that right: he said we *need* worms in our guts.

I looked at that bearded man and wondered what planet he had come from. The picture on his website showed penetrating eyes, a tie, and an official white jacket that proclaimed in a stately voice: "I am an authority." When we had our video chat, he was dressed more casually but was still all business. His office was prim and proper, with tidy wooden shelves and a neat array of photographs. I had checked his background. This man is the head of an entire laboratory at Duke University—a lab that helped discover the purpose of a mysterious little organ known as the appendix.[13]

"All worms are labeled as parasites, which is wrong," he said, bringing my eyes back to focus on his. "It's similar to what we thought in the late 1800s about bacteria: they are all bad." Okay, he admitted, some do cause problems, but what really got his dander up was the label "parasite" and how that one word leads to a way of thinking. "It is human nature—we see a person of a certain

---

[13] In some animals, the cecum is the safe haven for microbes. In humans, the appendix hangs off the cecum like a worm with nowhere to go and serves as a deep, dark shelter for a secret stash of microbes.

look and appearance do something bad and we think everybody with that look and appearance is bad."

I get that. That knee-jerk perspective is at the core of so many problems.

"That's how humans survived so long, right?" he said. "We survive based on our biases."

Piper's got biases, too: She'll spring back from a garden hose, an instinctive reaction to a bias against something long and skinny in the grass. A bias that keeps her alive when the hose is a rattlesnake. This man, William Parker, was speaking deep truth.

"Sometimes, though," he said with a sigh, "they get us in trouble. We have this bias about worms."

A niggle of guilt crawled across the back of my skull. Those creatures in that possum—I had thrown my bias at them. But aren't they parasites?

William had wanted to know what worms can do for a human gut. With rats, you can feed them some worms and then go stirring around in their ceca. With people, it's not so simple.[14] So William had to work this problem backward. He tracked down self-treaters—people who treat their own medical condition by ingesting helminths[15]—and started asking questions:

Q1: Who are these people?
A1: Most are highly educated. Many have medical degrees.
Q2: What helminths are they using?
A2: Human hookworms, human whipworms, porcine (pig) whipworms, and rat tapeworms.

---

[14] How many people do you know who would willingly swallow worms for a scientific study?
[15] In the US, selling helminths is illegal, so self-treaters have found a few other options: turn to the black market, ship them in from overseas, or filch them off the feces of a friend.

Q3: What are they trying to cure?

A3: Just about any condition that involves inflammation.

When an invader enters your body, your immune system sends in an army to hack it, smack it, whack it dead. That army (cells, histamine, proteins, fluid, and more) causes redness, swelling, heat, pain . . . better known as inflammation.[16]

So why would a person infect themselves with parasites? Don't the helminths cause inflammation?

There's this hypothesis that helminths actually reduce inflammation. Here's how Erin had described it: "The way that helminths stay in your gut is to produce proteins that kind of calm the immune system. They are just kind of like, 'Shhhh, it's okay for me to be here,' right?" So, basically, helminths have been tricking our immune systems for forever.

Then along came modern sanitation and medicines that kill off the worms. Bye-bye helminths. Suddenly there's nothing calming the immune system. There's nothing preventing inflammation.

"So now, the immune system is like, '*Yes*, full power! Wait! What am I doing full power for? What am I looking for? Then it sees pollen and says '*You*! You are the intruder!'" This could be why so many people in the modern world have allergies. It could also explain why some people's immune systems are attacking their own bodies. What it comes down to, Erin said, is "chronic systemic inflammation of your body attacking itself because it is no longer being calmed by helminths."

Whoa.

Chronic = happens all the time.

---

[16] Even something as small as a drip of mosquito spit causes your skin to balloon up.

Systemic = happens all over the body.

Inflammation = just the sound of that word makes my body hurt.[17]

Scary stuff that we call autoimmune diseases.

While William was collecting all that information from surveys, a science writer mentioned some self-treaters who claimed their depression was going away.

William told me, "The first thing I thought was, 'That's stupid. That's not right.' Of course, it only takes 2 seconds to do a Google search and realize—*Whoa!*" Inflammation plays a role in many nervous system disorders (depression, anxiety, multiple sclerosis, etc.).

When he made the connection between depression and brain swelling, his thinking took a U-turn: "This is not so stupid. This might make sense."

For his studies, William needed to recruit a brain scientist. He found one who had been using rats to test out drugs for mental diseases. When he explained the study to her, she laughed and said, "'Yeah, well, we've known for a long time that if your rat colonies get pinworm infections, your experiments stop working.'"

Wait a second.

"So, she already knew it was gonna work, because it is common knowledge in the field, if you get an intestinal worm [in rats you are using for a test], you no longer get neuroinflammation, which causes these disorders."

What!? And they ignored that result?

"They knew this for decades! Just never published it."

---

[17] We're not talking about when you twist your ankle and it swells for a day or two. That kind of inflammation helps you heal. This kind, hidden so far inside that you can't see it or maybe even feel it, can be evil.

"The worm destroyed their experiment?" I asked.

"Right, right, right," William said. "If your animals aren't sick, then you can't try your drug. HA! This is the key: they never learned from it."

"Obviously, you did."[18]

William's studies found: "If a baby rat is born to a mother with intestinal worms, the baby's brain is protected from inflammation—boom!" His fingers show the explosion that happened in his brain.

Could the same thing work in people?

A couple of months after talking with William, I found another dead possum. Pulling her off the road, I watched a white-pink worm crawling out of her mouth. He was being evicted from the only home he'd ever known.

When the possum lost her life, what happened to the entire ecosystem within?

Who is this worm? Where can he hope to go? And where, exactly, did he come from? I toted the possum body home and took a closer look.

I found all the worm's BFFs nestled in the possum's tummy. They reminded me of earthworms. Farther down in the intestines were longer, grayer worms. Even farther along, in the cecum, were tiny tubes less than a centimeter long and as clear as cellophane.

My forceps grabbed one of the segmented gray worms—a tapeworm as flat as a shed snakeskin.

Under the scope, a tapeworm is lustrous, like a string of pearls.

---

[18] Something else we might want to learn from: In a 4.5-year study, 12 people who had multiple sclerosis *and* had helminths showed fewer relapses and symptoms than MS patients with no parasites. Plus, when the helminths were eliminated, the MS got worse.

If you think about it, these creatures are extraordinary. The body is so simple—just a head and a neck and a lo-o-o-ng stretch of segments[19]—yet they can thrive inside almost any vertebrate on the planet. Elephants, foxes, leopards, iguanas, fish—yep. At least 4,810 types of tapeworm are known to science, and a recent study just found 215 more![20] Some look like stacked doughnuts, others like alien ships.

They survive without a mouth, a butt, or a gut. Or maybe I should say their entire body is their gut. It's like they *are* a gut turned inside out. The surface of their body is covered in micro-triches, fine filaments that reach out to absorb nutrients.[21] Imagine swimming in a pool of milkshake and being able to drink through every inch of your skin.

With an electron microscope, someone zoom-zoomed in on a collection of microtriches. Just like scales on mammal hairs, the variety of shapes mesmerized me: fringed like an oriental rug, pointy as a shrew's nose, buttressed like the base of a tree, fuzzy as a baby's warm head, scaly as pangolin skin, reaching like sala-mander toes, tangled as sunlit spiderwebs.

Why have I never known their beauty? Do we have to label them "parasite"? Is it really all so black and white? I'm finding it hard to believe they always take and never give back. Doesn't every relationship include some of both?

---

[19] Pythons, go home! A tapeworm from a sperm whale is one of the longest animals on earth. At 98 feet, this tapie is longer than 3 reticulated pythons strung tongue to tail.

[20] To make those discoveries, a scientific team spent 8 years scouring the bowels of the earth. One of their favorite finds looked like Dr. Seuss's Cat in the Hat, so they named it *Seussapex!*

[21] They might also help the worms stay put in the stream of sloshing food and give them a clue about what's going on around them (tapies have no ears, eyes, or noses, you know!).

Maybe helminths aren't good,[22] *and* helminths aren't bad.[23] Maybe they are just another piece of the intricate ecosystem inside a body.

Should we use helminths as medicine? The answer is not clear. Even William Parker says they aren't a silver bullet. One thing I am clear about: we need to pull out our lenses and keep looking at this.[24] Every time we turn away from something like worms in the gut or pumping poo up into someone's colon or tough questions about animal extinction, we miss out.

Like Joe Roman had told me so many months ago, "In science, rarely do you get a yes or a no." This is the evolution of understanding. This is scientific knowledge in the making. What we do with that new knowledge is a choice each of us gets to make.

---

[22]One helminth can cause rectal prolapse. That's when part of your large intestine pops out of your heinie. Ouch!

[23]A helminth is being tested to help people with peanut allergies.

[24]Some scientists think we can isolate the chemicals helminths excrete and use that as medicine? Worm poo to the rescue? Not exactly. For example, because they have no gut, tapeworms don't produce feces. They do produce waste; they just don't have an anus for it to slide out of. ☺

CHAPTER 14
GOLDMINE

Poop could be a goldmine—literally. Engineers are mining human sewage sludge to find gold (and platinum and silver and . . .).

Why is there gold in sewage? It's used in medicine and dentistry.[1] What goes in must come out! Sewage sludge also contains factories' feces (i.e., the drippings and drainage from all their efforts). Gold is used to make lots of things: electronic connectors in cell phones,[2] windows that reflect solar radiation, lubrication for spaceship parts, etc.

Environmental engineer Paul Westerhoff from Arizona State University told me, "In the sludge of every million people, there's probably several million dollars of gold and silver."

Several million dollars!! But, hey, it's not like there are bars of gold floating in that stew. It's more like flecks. Think of all the digging you'd have to do—there's a reason why no one is sludge diving.

What all that sewage is full of, Paul said, is dead bodies. Not

---

[1] If your mouth made so little spit you couldn't speak, eat, or swallow, you'd thank the Polish company that figured out that gold makes artificial saliva work right.
[2] A cell phone contains 50¢ worth of gold.

human bodies! Dead bodies of bacteria. "That's what these bio-solids are."

Biosolids? That took my mind way, way back to the poop train.

"At that point, it is not really poo anymore," Paul carried on. "A wastewater treatment plant is like your gut." Bacteria live on the nitrogen and carbon. They chew it on down and what's left are dead bacterial cell bodies.

"About half of the biosolids in the US go to land application—tree farms, cotton fields, Home Depot—"

"What?!"

"—Class A biosolids. You can buy them at Lowes, Home Depot. It means they have been composted for a certain amount of time to kill viruses or pathogens."

You can buy this stuff? Paul's not waiting for my mind to catch up. He plows on. "About 40 percent of the biosolids go to landfills."

I'm imagining an infinite line of cartoon train cars. Dump. Dump. Dump. All that nasty filling up Alabama's earth.

But this engineer's painting a different picture.

"Every night a landfill has to cover the municipal garbage waste with a layer of soil. That layer prevents birds from eating it, prevents it from blowing away, prevents aerosols from coming out." He pauses. "They need to get it from somewhere."

So, landfills need sewage?

"And there is actually energy in those bacterial cells."

A yellow-and-black machine wedges into view. With a 13-foot-wide scoop held in front like a fiddler crab's claw, it pushes and piles. With 2 wheel-like drums sporting 400 solid steel teeth, it grinds.

"A Tana compactor," says Shawn Luker. "That thing weighs 129,000 pounds and it is chewing everything." From under his camo cap, Shawn watches reverently as it moves across the surface. Push, churn, pulverize—all controlled by a pair of joysticks.

We're sitting in a pickup truck, perched on a mountainous mound of trash. Shawn is the manager of the Morgan County Regional Landfill.

A stretch of green garden hose, a hunk of pink insulation, a bent basketball hoop. Black bags, white bags, blue bags.[3] A bright blue kiddie pool, mashed pancake-flat. In this landfill, lifeless waste waits for a secret ingredient.

Up wheels a white truck. Then, back, back, back it goes. The bed raises to an angle not much different from Piper's when she's assumed the position.[4] It excretes black gold—biosolids from the local sewage plant. The black obliterates all that color, but only for a moment. The compactor powers in again, churning in the biosolids. Like a mouth, it grinds and mashes, kneading richness into the inorganic waste.

This landfill is putting human poop to work.

Later we watch a new landfill cell being prepared. It's as wide as a farmer's field. Black cylinders wait expectantly on orange dirt. They look like rolls of trash bags but are the length of a truck. That material will seal the bottom, sides, and top of the cell. After the trash, trees, and poop are dumped in, methane makers will get to gobbling, then fart out gas. The black seal will make sure none escapes.

My eyes find a cell that is already filled and sealed. Black tubes

---

[3] Shawn despises plastic grocery bags that parachute across the landfill and look trashy.
[4] Have you ever tried squatting, instead of sitting? It changes the angle and helps some people out. Learn more in the annotated bibliography.

sprout from the top.[5] Shawn and I follow them to a building housing a mustard-yellow machine the size of a bedroom.

The oily smell makes my nose twitch. My ears are crowded with the whine and whirl and continuous clatter. Once we step outside, the machine's operator tells me it's the same engine they use in a locomotive train.[6]

Just what does that methane-breathing machine do? Convert it into a little something we call electricity. This landfill generates enough electricity to power 1,000 homes a year.

Poop to power—now that's my kind of goldmine!

One steamy July evening almost a year earlier, I had driven down to *the* landfill, the one the poop train was headed to. I stood digging my toe into the grit at the side of the road. I gazed past a chain-link fence, out over a field of pines all the size of my thigh, toward the giant that was ingesting all that poop.

Then along came a guy in a pickup truck, a neon vest, and two days of chin stubble. He kindly escorted me off the property.

I wasn't doing anything wrong, I promise. Just standing there, taking pictures, jotting notes, wondering why they were so willing to take in trainloads of feces. Did poop pay that well? I had even called ahead to ask permission, but no one returned my call. All that bad press must have made them nervous. And they should be nervous, right? They were dumping all that sludge into Alabama's earth!

But now, after talking to Paul and Shawn, after thinking about

---

[5] Without those pipes sucking out the methane, pressure would build up. Add in heat from fermentation, and you could get an underground fire.
[6] Trains mostly use diesel instead of methane as their power source.

bias, I got up my gumption and called again. And again and again. One day, I got through. The day after Memorial Day, I had a date to meet the vice president of the landfill.

"John Click?" I poke my head into the office. A lean man in Carhartts with rugged good looks strides toward me.

He gives a curt nod. "You must be Heather."

The air between us almost prickles. Me, the animal lover with a bird pendant hanging from my neck. Him, the trophy hunter with real heads hanging from his wall. Me, eager to talk about the poop train. Him, weary of defending his company, his job, his live-lihood from the backlash.

After the pleasantries adults always insist on, we climb into his truck to go see some biosolids.

Mr. Click tells me they built this landfill on an old coal mine. We pull up to the base of a massive hill, one of the completed land-fill cells. He explains that once they seal a cell, they need to get something growing on it, or else the soil will wash down into the river and then everyone, *everyone* will jump on their case.

"Here's my problem," he says. "All I got out here is rocky dirt from a strip mine." He points to our right. "As you can see, this was a holler that the coal mines left behind." It is nothing like the happy holler that possum came from.

To mine coal from the surface, first, you scrape the soil aside; second, you blast the rocks apart; third, you shove it all into a slag pile. While you are breaking up the coal and trucking it off to make electricity, the slag sits there for months. Rain runs the nutrients off it and into the river; the sun scorches out all hope of life.

The "holler" he points to is a gouge filled with gray rock from the size of a pea to a pickup truck. Most of it is barren-looking gravel that even ants wouldn't want to call home.

144

"Get grass to grow on that," Mr. Click says.

Then we face the hill in front of us. "You see all the nice pretty green?" He pulls off his shades and looks me in the eye. "That's biosolids."

We stroll out into the sloping meadow. Waist-high plants wave under my outstretched arms. A bumblebee *bzz-bzzs* on a purple flower. I lean over to peer at a bunny's tunnel through the grass. Some plant releases a fresh, fragrant smell.

This is a landfill?

"You are standing on biosolids," John says. He tilled them into the ground just like you do in a garden. And then he told me what germinated . . . tomatoes.

My brow arches up.

"So, when we first spread this with the grass seed, the first plants that were coming up were: tomatoes"—he counts these out on his fingers—"cucumbers, watermelon, even some gourd seeds, which I thought was very interesting. I was like, who's eating gourd seeds?"[7]

I almost say, "Mastodons," but keep my mouth shut because he's started in on another story.

Last summer the state environmental agency had come out to test the operation. "So, we are out here and it's a midsummer day, and you see little red balls all over the hillside."

"No way!" I look up and picture an entire garden of tomatoes coating the hill.

And the environmental scientist said, "You can eat these tomatoes."

---

[7] Pretty phenomenal that seeds survive the sewage treatment process. But then again, seeds evolved to survive the slippery trip through a gut.

Mr. Click was like, "I don't know about eatin' 'em."[8]

She said if the plant is healthy enough to produce a big juicy fruit, the fruit is healthy—as edible as any other.

"Now, the EPA does not allow you to farm vegetables on biosolids, but I think it is because—and it was her thought, too—people are too afraid."

Read the reports about food grown on biosolids, and it's like watching a tennis match:

- Warning! Warning! Earthworms living in biosolids soil end up with human medicine and fake fragrances in their bodies.
- No problem: In Germany, almost all biosolids are applied to farmland. Those folks aren't dead.
- Warning! Warning! Soil treated with biosolids contains more antibiotic-resistant genes.
- No problem: The compounds in biosolids are less toxic than table sugar.

We climb back in the truck and head up the dirt road. This man used to be a coal miner, so I tell him both my granddads were. Coal mines are the reason both my parents had food on their plates growing up. Driving up a slight grade, he's telling me how he used to play here as a kid, back when there were woods—TURKEY! The 2-foot hen struts across our path; her feathers shimmer like an earthy rainbow: beaver brown, foxy orange, the bronze of a pangolin.

---

[8] Remember Mr. Madison who lived by the train track in Parrish and who wanted to plant his garden? What would he think about that?

We pull up to the water catchment pond where the landfill and biosolids drain. It's where they test to make sure nothing's leaking or leaching out.[9]

This is no muddy pond. The water actually looks inviting. The trill of a treefrog has me looking for amphibian eggs in the water. A beaver's been busy stashing branches underwater. The lemon yellow of a dead insect catches my eye. You'd think a dead body would set off alarm bells in my brain: pollution, pollution, POLLUTION! But this mayfly body shouted, clean, clean, CLEAN!

Mayflies live underwater when they are kids. They dance around, waving feathery gills to get plenty of oxygen. When they grow up, they crawl out, split their skin, and get wings. They shed one more time and fly off to mate, lay eggs, and die. They may live only one day as an adult.[10]

Dead mayfly adults = everything's normal

There's more to it than that. When I go to test water quality, I look for mayflies. Mayfly kids are picky about their water. Dump in pollution and the population plummets. No way they'd ever survive to be grown-ups. By seeing an adult, I could infer the water wasn't full of waste.

---

[9] A short list of nasties that could seep out: arsenic (from rat poison), mercury (from batteries), cadmium (from electronic devices). Good reasons to never dump those cancer-causers in a dump.

[10] It's a pretty busy day, but since they don't have mouths, they don't have to waste time on a pit stop!

Someone had sent a paddleboat to the landfill, but John Click hadn't let that go to waste. It sat at the edge of the pond. "We picnic and we bass fish," he says. His kids swim here. I imagine him throwing in a line, his kids splashing around, scaring off all the fish. He's kind of ticked a beaver's chopped down his shade tree. I want to give his kids my favorite book on beavers.

He wants to show me another part of the landfill. We go up, up, up. This is 4-wheel-drive country. John nudges the nose of the truck over the crest of a hill. Before us, as far as I can see, is yellow brown. Dry slopes dotted with stunted trees.

"This is a 30-year-old coal mine," he says. It was reclaimed (the hole filled in and replanted) way back when John was a baby, but the trees are only as big as shrubs.

Why haven't they grown? Where are the rest of the trees? And what about the woodpeckers, the salamanders, the treefrogs?

"See how there is no soil?"

Things click into place in my brain. "No organic matter."

"No soil to grow nothing on, so the only way the soil is getting built up is the plant dies and it turns back into soil."

John's arm swinging wide has me taking in the expanse of it all. The soil is hard and hopeless.

"So, you are talking about, I'm thinking 50 to 100 years before you get any kind of soil layer," he says. "That's why it was our idea to take this land and use the biosolids."

The other side of the hill, the one we just climbed, is a wall of green.

As I step into it, the soil feels spongy under my feet. "This holds in the moisture," he says, kicking his boot heel into the dirt. "The biosolids. Ah, that's such a good dirt."

There are blackberries about to be ripe, goldenrod turning

sunlight into cellulose, and a nice brown pile of animal scat. Someone is making use of this fertile soil.

I squat and run my fingers through the dark soil, through poop from New York City. As I inhale that earthy aroma, an idea settles into place in my mind: this land was in need of a fecal transplant.

Then something sinks in a little deeper. Sure, humans can make a huge mess of things—we pollute the water, change the atmosphere, cause extinctions—but I had let those things cloud my vision. People aren't parasites on this planet. Human poop belongs here, in the soil, just as much as whale poop or coon poop or even helminth poop.[11]

A few minutes later, John crouches under a wild plum tree. His hand on the mud-covered trunk, his arm pointing down a game trail, his utter awe for the animal spelled out in the tone of his voice. Then we stand, separated by the branches of the plum tree, brought together by what we put in our mouths.

The plum's skin pops.

The tart juice runs.

The grin passes between us.

There's nothing like standing on a hillside with a new friend, feeding on the fruit of the earth, all thanks to the glories of poop.[12]

It isn't animal lover versus landfill guy. It's not Alabama versus New York, rural versus city, or good versus bad. Every single one of us is a living, breathing, *excreting* piece of this puzzle—the ever-evolving ecosystem we call Earth.

---

[11] Just because tapeworms can't go #2, nothing's stopping roundworms. I wonder if they have their own microbiome.

[12] Thank you, New York City!

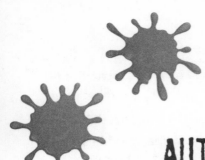

AUTHOR'S NOTE

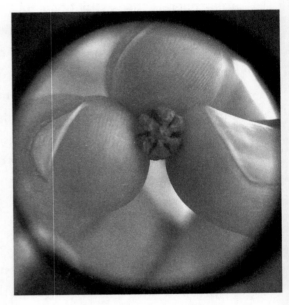

Intricate and elegant, the eraser-sized sculpture captivates me. Its shape reminds me of the day I made snow angels with my cousins. Its green radiates the joy of a vibrant spring day. Its odor, grassy and good, takes me back to camp, standing nose to muzzle with a horse.

If you picked up this caterpillar poop, you might have a different reaction. Why am I so drawn to it? By now you know poop has its own kind of magic. But even before I knew the value of poo, insect frass[1] had its own special place in my heart. For some reason, insects—and everything about them—speak to me like no other creatures on the planet. You know people who are crazy about snakes or dinosaurs or cute, cuddly pandas. Well, I've got a bug bias.

---

[1] Yep, entomologists (insect scientists) have their own term for poop.

Bias. That word is so strong, so potent. In science, we work to scrub every ounce of bias out of our studies. Like Kat and her transect lines, we work hard to make sure our samples are not biased. Like Erin and her wormy rats, we know that other scientists will examine our methods for bias. Like Joe and his big idea about whale pumps, we cast our studies out into the world where other scientists will question our interpretations. As scientists, we are trained to be skeptical. Even with all that, science still includes bits of bias.

Just like every part of this book includes bias.

Don't get me wrong, none of the facts in this book are fiction, but a human had to select those facts. My brain filtered through thousands of tasty tidbits to decide which to plip-plop into the book. Every human brain has its own bias based on its experience. Five years ago, I would never have included the helminth story that questioned traditional medicine. My mother was a nurse. My degree is in biology. Recently, though, I spent a year in pain from an unrelenting injury. The medical profession had no answers; I turned to alternative medicine.[2] See how that experience biased my selection? Every story is biased. It is, after all, created by a human brain.

Bias isn't always a bad thing. In this world of information overload, bias helps us select what to pay attention to. When we ignore bias, though, that's when things can turn ugly. Interacting with the world, we need to be on the lookout for bias in science, in books, in ourselves.

Once, I read a scientific study about how polar bears aren't

---

[2] Don't worry, I'm okay now. It was just a rough year.

starving. What? Those great white beasts aren't on a one-way trip to extinction? I was ecstatic! You may have heard how, as our planet warms up, polar bears are losing their icy perches. So, they are spending their summers on land, with no gushy seals to eat. The word was, they were starving. When I read about a scientist who sleuthed through 642 piles of polar bear scat and found mushrooms, caribou, fish, and all kinds of other food, I knew, *just knew* polar bears were saved.

But the scientists weren't actually saying that. My brain had jumped to a conclusion I wanted to hear. The scientists' conclusion was that the bears are adapting to the food available. Is that food enough? Does roaming around to track down the food use up too much energy? Will the bears survive? We don't know.

This study does give me hope for those great white beasts, but this story reminds me to watch out for my own bias. When I wander in the woods, I need to wear poop goggles. When I wander in the world, I need to wear bias goggles.

Do me a favor: strap on your own goggles and join me in making a few more discoveries!

FECAL FUN FOR YOU

Poop is everywhere! And that means you are surrounded by scientific potential. Dig out a pencil, rev up your curiosity, and go make some discoveries!

WHICH WAY?

A scientific study found that when it is time to "go," dogs line themselves up with the earth's magnetic field. Grab a compass and a note pad. Walk one dog for a week or visit a dog park and record your observations. Do dogs pee and poop facing north or south but not east or west? What else might affect this? Weather? Slope of the ground? Individual dogs' preferences?

SNOOP ON POOP

In the spring, find a bird's nest with chicks. With binoculars, observe the nest for 15 minutes. How many times do Mom and Pop Bird fly in? Are they carrying food? How many times do they fly out? Are they carrying a little white pouch? That's poop from the chicks![1] Can you estimate the size of the fecal sac? Can you calculate the rate at which the chicks are pooping?

---

[1] A chick's poop comes out wrapped in a mucus membrane. Mom or Dad may munch on those feces—remember, a newborn doesn't have many microbes, so the poo is mostly undigested food. Once the chick grows and the poo is full of microbes, the parents carry the disposable diapers away and ditch them.

READY, SET, GO!

A group of scientists timed how long it took different mammals to poop. Pandas, piggies, puppies—they all took about 12 seconds to go. Why is that? How is that possible? Pull out a stopwatch and record an animal near you. To get a valid average, aim for 10 observations. Don't have any pets? You are a mammal, too![2]

---

[2] My average was 16 seconds. Piper's was 10.7. Annie was too shy to participate!

POO-TENTIAL

Here are a few other true uses of poo I couldn't stand to leave out.

- Astroplastic: When you are halfway to Mars and stranded without the right size wrench, what can you do? Put poo to use. Canadian college students figured out how to grow plastic from astronaut poop.[1] Dump that plastic into a 3D printer and—poof!—make just what you need. Other inventors are dreaming and scheming of using it to shield astronauts from space radiation or grow them gooey food! Eeeew.

- Pest Patrol: If a movie character saved thousands of lives by preventing an explosion, you would call them the hero. Here in the real world, we call them pest technicians. When pest techs visit a food-packaging plant, they send up a drone to search for rodent poo and save us all from distressful diarrhea. When they visit a nuclear power plant, the poo may clue them in to where mice have been gnawing insulation off electrical wires. Bare wires lead to short circuits. Short circuits can lead to . . . *Kaboom*!

- New Knees: An expert on human bone health used dinosaur doo-doo instead of bones in a medical experiment. Why? He knew it would grab the media's attention—attention his earlier results failed to get. And if he could get the word

---

[1] Most plastics are long chains of molecules made from the carbon in fossil fuels. These students thought, Why not use the carbon in poo? They added DNA from one bacteria into another and let it grow plastic. Upcycling at its best.

spread, his results could revolutionize the world of human joint replacements.

- Poop to Power: In Mississippi, poultry poop powers a 270,000-chicken farm; in Washington State, 3,000 cows poop out enough manure to power 300 homes; and over in the UK, a bus ran on human sewage. The bus could cruise 37 miles on a single person's annual waste (poop and food).
- Babysitter: At the Dallas Zoo, a mother hippo—whose first baby died just after birth, whose mate died last fall, who could easily have never become a mother again—got pregnant. Would this baby make it? How could zookeepers keep tabs on the baby's health during the pregnancy? Metabolites in Mom's feces. Thanks to those poo clues, there's one more megamuncher adding poop to the planet!

WONDERFUL WASTE WORDS

Poop comes in so many fun forms and has inspired so many fun words! Grow your vocabulary with this list (but don't forget to mind your manners)!

Biosolids	Sewage sludge that has been processed
BM	Bowel movement (produced when the bowels move poop out of the body)
Coprolite	Fossilized poop
Coprophagy	Feeding on feces
Dingleberry	A piece of poop that clings to an animal's anus
Droppings	Bird poop (but used more widely)
Dung	Herbivore poop
Excrement	Waste excreted from the body (particularly solid waste)
Feces	Scientific word for poop (term used in North America)
Faeces	Scientific word for poop (term used everywhere except North America)
Floaters	Poop that floats in the toilet
Frass	Insect and spider poop
Guano	Bat and seabird poop
In fimo	Poop examined scientifically
Loo	Toilet (especially in Britain)
Night soil	Human poop from chamber pots (used at night before indoor plumbing)
Ordure	What they called poop back in the 1700s
Patty	A round, flat piece of feces (like what a cow makes)

Pseudofeces	Fake poop from bivalves (clams, mussels, oysters)[1]
Scat	General word for poop, also used specifically for carnivore poop
Scatology	The study of scat
Sinker	Dense poop that sinks in the toilet
Stool	A medical term for feces
Thunderbox	Australian word for toilet

---

[1] When bivalves slurp in seawater, in addition to food they also get sand, grit, and (sadly) microplastic. They wrap that in mucus and—*ptooey*—spit it back out.

POOP SLEUTHS

All across the globe, people are becoming poop sleuths. High in the Himalayas, climbers attempting to summit a 20,000-foot peak pause their adventure to collect samples of poop from blue sheep. Over in Australia, every day folks snap pictures or scoop up echidna droppings from their backyards. On a college campus in North Carolina, volunteers collect a microbe that poops gold. All these citizens send their samples to scientists who put the poop to work.

Young people get in on the action, too! Among the honking cars and roaring trains of New York City, high school students help scientists track coyote populations through their poo.[1] Near Denver, Colorado, middle school students tweeze their way through clods of bison dung, looking for beetles. Bison used to roam those grasslands; dung beetles used to recycle their dung. Then humans moved in and bison moved out. No one paid any attention to the lowly beetles till we reintroduced bison into the area. Now, the dung isn't disappearing fast enough.[2] Do we need to reintroduce dung beetles? Which ones? How many? Scientists need help collecting the data. Australian students gather samples from ringtail possums. Are wild animals carrying antibiotic-resistant bacteria? Have our drugs slipped down the sewers, out

---

[1] Coyotes who never used to live in NYC now hide out in parks in the Bronx and Queens. Wily coyotes slipped in and took over the role wolves used to fill, keeping the rodent and raccoon populations in check.

[2] One species of dung beetle can pull 1,141 times its weight. If it was the size of a human, it could pull a northern right whale!

into the wild waters, and up into an animal's esophagus? Students are scooping up answers.

Last but not least, people donate their own stool.[3] I swiped some scat from my toilet and mailed it to the world's largest gut microbiome citizen science effort, the American Gut Project.[4] They ID the microbes from stool and make hypotheses about human health. No surprise, they found that if you are taking antibiotics, the diversity in your microbiome takes a nosedive. The surprise was that folks who weren't taking any medication also had antibiotics in their stool. Where did it come from? Must be from the cows and chickens they ate. That's the food chain for you!

Want to be a citizen scientist, too? Do your own research and find the perfect project for you. A good place to start is www.scistarter.com.

---

[3] Note: it takes a fecal and a financial donation—all those tests aren't cheap.
[4] Hope I used the right address!

ANNOTATED BIBLIOGRAPHY

I decided not to bore you with the actual "Works Cited" list as it is a billion entries long. (To see the entire list, visit my website, www .HeatherLMontgomery.com.) But the research for this book was SO MUCH FUN, I had to share some of this awesomeness.

Most of the book is based on my experiences and interviews. Too bad you can't road trip to visit all those homes, labs, and field sites, but you can check out these books, links, and videos. Surf on over—you'll be glad cyberspace isn't scratch-and-sniff![1]

CHAPTER 1: HUNK OF TONGUE

"Sequencing Reveals Mixed Ancestry for Wolves." *YouTube*, American Association for the Advancement of Science, 27 July 2016, www .youtube.com/watch?v=gWYFO6n22yo&feature=youtu.be.
Come on, admit it, you want to know what kind of information Dr. vonHoldt is going to get from that coyote tongue . . . Here's a video that sums up her study—the mind-blowing idea that maybe, just maybe, the endangered red wolf isn't actually a "real" species.
Sun, Catherine (@catsunbear). "#SciencePoop-Twitter Search." Twitter, 3 Feb. 2017, twitter.com/search?q=%23SciencePoop&src=typd.
Twitter? Yes, I actually used Twitter as a resource. A few of my favorite hashtags: #SciencePoop, #PoopScience, #WhosePoo. Pop on over, and you can learn how to dry salamander poo. Or see what happens when a poop stirrer goes out of control . . .

---

[1] When they do figure out how to make virtual poo smell, will we be able to turn the volume down?

Mattoni, Camilo I., et al. "Scorpion Sheds 'Tail' to Escape: Consequences and Implications of Autotomy in Scorpions (Buthidae: Ananteris)." *Plos One*, vol. 10, no. 1, 28 Jan. 2015, doi:10.1371/journal.pone .0116639.
So you can see what the severed stump of a scorpion's tail looks like.

CHAPTER 2: POOPY PUZZLE

Foreman, Alison. "In a Glamorous Turn of Events, Polar Bears Are Pooping Glitter to Fight off Extinction." *Mashable*, Mashable, 2 Mar. 2019, mashable.com/article/polar-bear-glitter-poop-cincinnati-zoo/.
Leave it to zookeepers to make glitter poop a *thing*. When you have the world's largest collection of polar bear poo, a little glitzy color coding goes a long way to keeping the samples straight.

From my dissection of bat guano: The "knob" and "saddle" that I determined to be an insect eye.

"Woman's Story Goes Viral Following Moose Poop Peddling Pitch." KSAT 12, 28 Sept. 2018, www.youtube.com/watch?v=Y2hOZEGa3I8.
Just in case you are curious about the poo-poo clock, turdy earrings, or fecal people.
Abrahams, Marc. "Researcher Invents Weapons of Waste Destruction." *The Guardian*, Guardian News and Media, 3 Sept. 2012, www

.theguardian.com/education/2012/sep/03/improbable-research
-waste-weapon-system.

Want to see a diagram of that poop gun?

Jones, Nicola. "Case Closed: You Can't Make a Knife Out of Frozen
Poop." *SAPIENS*, Wenner-Gren Foundation for Anthropological
Research, 17 Sept. 2019, www.sapiens.org/archaeology/poop-knife
-frozen/.

Up north, an old man was stranded on the ice without any tools, so he
molded his poop into a knife, used it to kill a dog, and survived. You
don't remember that story from the chapter? I wanted to include it,
but I double-check my facts and it didn't make the cut. I did find this
record of a scientist who put his own stuff to the test to fight this bit
of fake news.

CHAPTER 3: POO-POO CHOO-CHOO

Tagg, Andrew, et al. "Everything Is Awesome: Don't Forget the LEGO."
Journal of Paediatrics and Child Health, 22 Nov. 2018. *Wiley Online
Library*, doi:10.1111/jpc.14309.

This LEGO-swallowing study was awesome! Complete with a diagram of
LEGO head dimensions, a graph of FART scores, and—bonus—I was
able to understand it on the first read-through. Warning: There's a
reference to a four-letter word. And don't miss: #dontforgetthelego!

"Ig Nobel Prizes." *Improbable Research*, 1 July 2019, www.improbable
.com/ig-about/.

One of my favorite sites for quirky science. Type *poop* into the search
box and you'll find stories of glow-in-the-dark poo, how dino poo
can improve knee surgery, and a spray called Poop-Freeze (use on
dog droppings to harden before you pick up).

Febreze, director. *Febreze Presents: Breathe Happy Parrish. YouTube*,
Febreze, 16 May 2018, www.youtube.com/watch?v=QBLwaEl1TkQ.

When a video is sponsored by a for-profit company, you better think
twice about using it as a source. I didn't depend on this video for
facts, but I did watch it to "meet" some of Parrish's residents before I
met them in person. In case you are wondering, it is a fact that
Febreze donated more than 1,000 bottles of air freshener to the
town.

"Global Diarrhea Burden | Global Water, Sanitation and Hygiene |
Healthy Water | CDC." *Centers for Disease Control and Prevention,*
Centers for Disease Control and Prevention, 17 Dec. 2015, www.cdc
.gov/healthywater/global/diarrhea-burden.html.

Ever try to find one accepted number for how many kids die of diarrhea?
Don't. Because no one's out there counting flushes, every number
you find is an estimate, and each estimate is based on different data.
So, who do you believe? I figured the Centers for Disease Control,
the organization created by the US of A to protect American health,
would be the ultimate source. Turns out, even the CDC quoted
someone else.

Earth, BBC, director. *Incredible "Toilet" Plant.* Performance by David
Attenborough, *YouTube,* YouTube, 9 Aug. 2013, www.youtube.com
/watch?v=TwL7K_loRjM.

Don't miss Sir David Attenborough's take on the symbiotic relationship
between the tree shrew and the toilet plant. (I told you research was
awesome!)

CHAPTER 4: DOGGIES AND DUNG

Elephant Parade Poo Poo Paper. YouTube, 30 Apr. 2014, www.youtube
.com/watch?v=P47w9KlOJCc.

Watch them cook and mix and squish (yes, with their bare hands!)
elephant dung into a poo ball, then turn it into paper. I wonder if
I can do that with cow pies.

Montgomery, Heather L., interview with Dr. Laura Metrione about her
fecal metabolite research, 22 Feb. 2018.

Understanding metabolites and how scientists study them was super
gnarly. Dr. Laura Metrione, who is like a metabolite detective,
jumped on the phone and helped me sort it all out. She works for the
South-East Zoo Alliance for Reproduction and Conservation. Zoos
ship her feces, and she ferrets out what the metabolites might mean.
Check out how they learn about gorilla personalities, giant river otters
as parents, and other poopy projects at www.sezarc.org/projects.

"Elephant Ivory Tracking." *Center for Conservation Biology*, University
of Washington, conservationbiology.uw.edu/research-programs
/elephant-ivory-tracking/.

Wasser, Samuel K., et al. "Combating Transnational Organized Crime by
Linking Multiple Large Ivory Seizures to the Same Dealer." *Science
Advances*, vol. 4, no. 9, 19 Sept. 2018, doi:10.1126/sciadv.aat0625.

Together this website and this scientific paper painted a picture of just
how Conservation Canines tracked down those poachers. Haunting
pics of elephant trunks, maps of poaching hotspots, and a you-are-
there video trailer complete with gun-packing good guys. On other
pages of their site, you can read all about the scat-detecting dogs!

CHAPTER 5: STOOL TO FUEL

The fire finally lights—but
mostly that's the newspaper.

"Nutrition Calculator & Information | McDonald's Canada." *McDonald's: Burgers, Fries & More. Quality Ingredients.*, www.mcdonalds.com/ca /en-ca/about-our-food/nutrition-calculator.html.

Don't believe me about cellulose in your shake? Good for you! Check the facts for yourself.

"Gasketeers on the BBC Evening News." Performance by Transition Malvern Hills, BBC, 29 Nov. 2010, www.youtube.com/watch ?v=wM6AlkttUGk.

Much of my information came from my interview with Brian Harper and deep research into the topic. You can get an overview (and hear those nifty British accents) in this news story.

Fleming, Nic. "From Stools to Fuels: The Street Lamp That Runs on Dog Do." *The Guardian*, 1 Jan. 2018, www.theguardian.com/environment /2018/jan/01/stools-to-fuels-street-lamp-runs-on-dog-poo-bio -energy-waste-.

Want to learn even more about those lamps that act as loos? How about the poo-powered bus? This article's got you covered.

CHAPTER 6: GOT GUTS?

McKenny, Erin. "Gut Microbes." *Do. Learn. Teach.*, sites.google.com /prod/view/doteachlearn/do/gut-microbes.

Dr. Erin McKenny taught me so much. Watch her teach other lemur scientists all about gut microbes.

"Got Guts?" *SciStarter*, scistarter.org/got-guts.

Calling all hunters! Here's your chance to contribute to poop science.

Montgomery, Heather L. "Journal Entry." Alabama, Ardmore, 20 Dec. 2018.

Writing a book requires lots and lots of prewriting. Pages and pages of words get trimmed down to paragraphs or sentences or even just phrases for the final published product. These are my original notes on the kingsnake dissection. Look how much got axed!

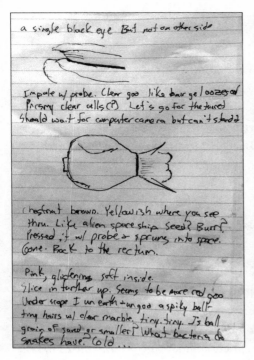

a single black eye But not on other side

Impale w/ probe. Clear goo like hair gel oozes or I'm sorry clear cells (?) Let's go for the tweel Should wait for computer camera but can't stand2

Chestnut brown. Yellowish where you see thru. Like alien space ship seed? Burr? Pressed it w/ probe a sprung into space. Gone. Back to the rectum.

Pink, glistening soft inside. Slice in further up. Seems to be more red goo Under scope I un earth + un goo a spiky ball- tiny hairs w/ clear marble. tiny. tiny. Is ball grain of sand or smaller? What bacteria do snakes have. Cold...

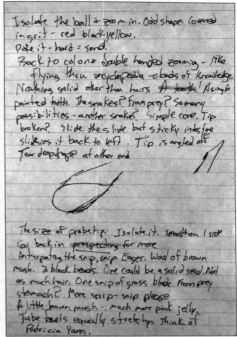

Isolate the ball + zoom in. Odd shape. Covered in grit - red black yellow. Poke it - hard = sand. Back to colon. Double handed zooming - like flying thru encyclopedia -clouds of knowledge Nothing solid other than hairs. A tooth! A single pointed tooth. The snakes? From prey? So many possibilities - another snake? Simple core. Tip broken? Slide the slide but sticky intestine slitheries it back to left. Tip is angled off Tear drop shape at other end

The size of probe tip. Isolate it. smoothen I see Go back in prospecting for more Anticipating the snip, snip. Eager. Wad of brown mush. a black beads. One could be a solid seed. Not as much hair. One snip of grass black. From prey stomach? More snip-snip please A little brown mush - much more pink jelly. Tube feels equally stretchy. Think of Patricia Yang.

GUT LENGTHS TO BODY LENGTHS

Animal Dissected	Gut Length (in)	Body Length (in)	Gut:Body Ratio
Beaver	333	27	12:1
Deer Fawn	167	~30	5.6:1
Kingsnake	63	44	1.4:1
River Otter	142	24	5.9:1

After chatting with Erin, I put all my gut data into a chart. Something looked odd. The gut-to-body length ratio of the fawn (an herbivore) was similar to that of the river otter (a carnivore). Erin explained it in a note: "That baby herbivore is actually, technically, a carnivore, because in a way it's eating its mother." Milk is all protein, sugar, and fat. A fawn (or a baby human) doesn't grow a long intestine or collect fiber-munching microbes until it stops nursing and switches to a grown-up diet.

Eschner, Kat. "This Man's Gunshot Wound Gave Scientists a Window into Digestion." *Smithsonian.com*, Smithsonian Institution, 6 June 2017, www.smithsonianmag.com/smart-news/grisly-story -human-guinea-pig-alexis-st-martin-180963520/.
The doctor who licked the stomach lining discovered acid isn't released till food jump-starts the digestive system.

CHAPTER 7: SURVIVAL

My visits with Lauren Guintini and Dr. Ari Grinspan gave me the stories for this chapter. These 3 videos brought those stories to life:
McKenna, Maryn. "Why Would Anyone Get a Fecal Transplant? Watch a Brother and Sister Explain." *National Geographic*, 22 June 2015, www .nationalgeographic.com/science/phenomena/2015/06/22/fmt-film/.
Don't just take my word for it, hear Lauren dish on what it's like to get that kind of gift from her brother.
News, WGBH, director. *Openbiome*. YouTube, 6 Apr. 2017, www.youtube .com/watch?v=gcWhR9ceY9c.
Little blue bowls, big brown bowel movements; this video took me inside the lab where they turn muck into medicine.
Arthur, Benjamin. *The Invisible Universe of the Human Microbiome*. *YouTube*, NPR, 5 Nov. 2013, www.youtube.com/watch ?v=5DTrENdWvvM.
Check out this 5-minute NPR video for a great overview on the microbiome.

CHAPTER 8: MORE FECES, PLEASE!

Live, BBC 5, director. *Thar She Blows! Diver Caught in Whale "Poonado."* *YouTube*, YouTube, 23 Jan. 2015, www.youtube.com/watch ?v=r4JJWuHmqPs.

Why do I love primary sources? Watch this video from the guy who was
swimming when he discovered the whale poonado—complete with
details about poo-flavored water dripping down into his mouth—and
you will understand my obsession.

DeMarco, Emily. "Watch: Penguins May Use Feces to Melt Snow off
Breeding Sites." *Science*, 27 Apr. 2015, www.sciencemag.org/news
/2015/04/watch-penguins-may-use-feces-melt-snow-breeding-sites
?rss=1.
Want to try your hand at helping scientists? If you like looking at
penguins and have access to the internet and permission from an
adult, you can help, too. Visit Penguin Watch at https://www
.zooniverse.org/projects/penguintom79/penguin-watch/.

Giaimo, Cara. "When the Western World Ran on Guano." *Atlas Obscura*,
Atlas Obscura, 14 Oct. 2015, www.atlasobscura.com/articles/when
-the-western-world-ran-on-guano.
Back in the 1800s, European farmers weren't the only ones who wanted a
few scoops. Americans begged for that guano goodness, too, so
Congress made it legal with the Guano Islands Act. From the official
record of the Acts of Congress:
"When any citizen or citizens of the United States may have discovered,
or shall hereafter discover, a deposit of guano on any island, rock or
key not within the lawful jurisdiction of any other government, and
not occupied by citizens of any other government, and shall take
peaceable possession thereof, and occupy the same, said island, rock
or key may at the discretion of the President of the United States, be
considered as appertaining to the United States . . ."
Read: Any US citizen can claim a poop-covered island for the USA.
Crazy! And, this act is still active. Want to go find us an island?

Holzman, David C. "As Big Animals Poop Out." *Science News for
Students*, 11 Dec. 2015, www.sciencenewsforstudents.org/article/big
-animals-poop-out.
Curious about megapoopers? This article has got what you need. Plus,
you get to see a fossilized glyptodont.

CHAPTER 9: PUMPKIN PIE

Reiserer, Randall S., et al. "Seed Ingestion and Germination in Rattlesnakes: Overlooked Agents of Rescue and Secondary Dispersal." *Proceedings of the Royal Society B: Biological Sciences*, vol. 285, no. 1872, 2018, p. 20172755., doi:10.1098/rspb.2017.2755.
Read how snake scientists literally dug into their research—all 22 stomachs and 42 intestines.
Kistler, Logan, et al. "Gourds and Squashes (*Cucurbita* spp.) Adapted to Megafaunal Extinction and Ecological Anachronism through Domestication." *Proceedings of the National Academy of Sciences*, vol. 112, no. 49, 8 Dec. 2015, pp. 15107–15112, doi:10.1073/pnas .1516109112.
Here's Logan's scientific paper, complete with a map, a chart, and a bar graph—love that geeky stuff!
Rossen, Jake. "How Mammoth Poop Gave Us Pumpkin Pie." *Mental Floss*, 12 Nov. 2018, mentalfloss.com/article/517145/how-mammoth -poop-gave-us-pumpkin-pie.
The awesomeness article that made me almost burn the pumpkin pie.
"Cancer-Fighting Condiment." *National Mustard Museum*, 18 Apr. 2014, mustardmuseum.com/cancer-fighting-condiment/.
Want to skip your veggies? Read this. Wait—can you trust them? They might be a bit biased . . .

CHAPTER 10: ALPHABET SOUP

"VTShorebirds." *VTShorebirds*, Virginia Tech, www.vtshorebirds.org/.
See the science and meet the peeps involved in the piping plover project.
Deedrick, Douglas W., and Sandra L. Koch. "Forensic Communications." *FBI*, July 2004, archives.fbi.gov/archives/about-us/lab/forensic

-science-communications/fsc/july2004/research/2004_03_research02 .htm.

What—you want to snoop on the FBI's document about hair? I thought so! Scroll on through for all the coolest patterns.

Barrios-de Pedro, et al. "Exceptional Coprolite Association from the Early Cretaceous Continental Lagerstätte of Las Hoyas, Cuenca, Spain." *Plos One*, vol. 13, no. 5, 23 May 2018, doi:10.1371/journal.pone .0196982.

Coprolites (fossilized feces) are cool! One problem: people in different places find them and give them different names. That's confusing. So, when 433 coprolites were found in one spot in Spain, Sandra Barrios-de Pedro created a dichotomous key to help everyone speak the same language. She made up names for them like *rosary, fir-tree,* and *bump-headed lace*!

CHAPTER 11: FECAL FLOATS

"Toronto Daredevil Raccoon Climbs 700-Ft Skyscraper." *CityNews Toronto*, 17 Apr. 2015, toronto.citynews.ca/2015/04/16/toronto -daredevil-raccoon-climbs-700-ft-skyscraper/.

See what we can learn from people who pay attention to poop!

Mitchinson, John, and John Lloyd. *The Book of Animal Ignorance: Everything You Think You Know Is Wrong*. New York: Harmony Books, 2007. Pages 173–174.

I read widely for my research (i.e., I get to read whatever I want, like this book with cool animal trivia!).

Maxey, Kirk M. "Lose Weight . . . and Your Poop Will Glow in the Dark Too!" *Kirk M. Maxey: Blog and Website*, 8 Nov. 2013, kirkmaxey.com /2013/11/08/lose-weight-and-your-poop-will-glow-in-the-dark-too/.

Here's the scoop on that glowing poop: Scientists engineered a gut-dwelling bacteria to release a molecule that signals you to feel full.

To test it, they fed the bacteria to rats. If the bacteria were healthy and doing their job, those rats should eat less. But how could the scientists know if the bacteria were thriving? Sneaky, sneaky—they inserted firefly DNA into the bacteria so that later, green glowing turds showed the poop-ulation was thriving inside.

"Woodrat Research." Performance by Gretchen Fowles, *Discover DEP-New Jersey Department of Environmental Protection*, YouTube, 30 Nov. 2018, www.youtube.com/watch?v=3dIrtG8Sxto.
Meet Gretchen Fowles and some Dumbo-eared cuties in this 2-minute video about the Allegheny woodrat project.

CHAPTER 12: PANDAS, POETRY, AND PALM OIL

Samuel and Audrey, director. *Poop Cafe in Seoul, Korea. Travel and Food Videos*, YouTube, 30 Aug. 2016, www.youtube.com/watch ?v=lsxLeclNbfo.
Want to take a virtual trip to the poop café? I thought so.
Craft, Lucy. "Japan's New Pop-up Poop Museum Proves a Hit." *CBS News*, CBS Interactive, 1 Apr. 2019, www.cbsnews.com/news/japan -poop-museum-proves-a-hit-in-yokahama/.
Japan takes the taboo out of poo. Visit the museum where you can stomp poo, lick an icky-awesome poo pop, or read one of the 4 million turdy textbooks.
Saying 'No' to Palm Oil Would Likely Displace, Not Halt Biodiversity Loss—IUCN Report. International Union for Conservation of Nature, 2018, www.iucn.org/news/secretariat/201806/saying-no-palm-oil -would-likely-displace-not-halt-biodiversity-loss—-iucn-report.
Not ready to swallow Dave's conclusion? Good. I like someone who is skeptical. Dave's still cranking numbers, but his team will contribute data in the future. For now, check out this IUCN summary and then dive into all 116 pages of the full report—if you dare.

CHAPTER 13: POOP AND PREJUDICE

Crew, Bec. "This Is Exactly What Happens When You Die." *ScienceAlert*, 3 Mar. 2016, www.sciencealert.com/watch-here-s-what-happens-when-you-die.

With a title like that, how could anyone resist? Warning: Mega-icky video!

Becker, Rachel. "Meet the Tapeworm Hunters Scouring Shark Guts for These 'Beautiful Little' Parasites." *The Verge*, The Verge, 22 Nov. 2017, www.theverge.com/2017/11/22/16691086/tapeworms-parasites-sea-food-raw-fish-meat-science-intestines-biodiversity.

When I surfed over to www.theverge.com, I spotted loaded language—*living noodles, infested guts, tapeworm hunting, fish entrails*—that lit my fact-checking radar up, but their record came back clean. Turns out they like to have fun with their facts (just like me)!

"As the Worm Turns." *This American Life*, performance by Patrick Walters, season 404: Enemy Camp, episode Act Three, 2 Apr. 2010, www.thisamericanlife.org/404/enemy-camp-2010/act-three.

Just why did Jasper Lawrence visit Cameroon to infest himself with hookworms? I probably would never have given his story a second chance, but this was RadioLab, one of my favorite NPR programs. Warning: The squishy sound effects are kind of creepy.

Williamson, Lauren L., et al. "Got Worms? Perinatal Exposure to Helminths Prevents Persistent Immune Sensitization and Cognitive Dysfunction Induced by Early-Life Infection." *Brain, Behavior, and Immunity*, vol. 51, Jan. 2016, pp. 14–28, doi:10.1016/j.bbi.2015.07.006.

Briggs, Neima, et al. "The Hygiene Hypothesis and Its Inconvenient Truths about Helminth Infections." *PLOS Neglected Tropical Diseases*, Public Library of Science, 15 Sept. 2016, journals.plos.org/plosntds/article?id=10.1371%2Fjournal.pntd.0004944.

Are helminths good or bad? Dig into these papers to scrutinize both sides of the issue for yourself.

Dixit, Aakanksha, et al. "Novel Therapeutics for Multiple Sclerosis
    Designed by Parasitic Worms." *International Journal of Molecular
    Sciences*, vol. 18, no. 10, 13 Oct. 2017, p. 2141, doi:10.3390
    /ijms18102141.
The results from that study on multiple sclerosis caught my eye. But did
    you notice the sample size? Of course you did, and you know 12
    patients is not enough. But does that mean the info is no good? They
    also compared prevalence of multiple sclerosis to the presence of
    human whipworm in different parts of the world. When plip-plopped
    down on a graph, every point hugged the x- or y-axis. Wherever
    whipworm has been wiped off the map (US, Belgium, Australia),
    multiple sclerosis is raging. Is that correlation or causation?
Chervy, Lenta. "Unified Terminology for Cestode Microtriches: A
    Proposal from the International Workshops on Cestode Systematics
    in 2002–2008." *Folia Parasitologica*, vol. 56, no. 3, 1 Sept. 2009,
    pp. 199–230, doi:10.14411/fp.2009.025.
Just in case you want to take a peek at those mesmerizing microtriches.

CHAPTER 14: GOLDMINE

Compactor, Tana. "TANA COMPACTOR." YouTube, 14 Apr. 2014, www
    .youtube.com/watch?v=3moDtJi11Cw.
Wanna watch a compactor chew down trash? This video's almost as
    good as being there beside it, and you get to skip the stink.
"Squatty Potty® Toilet Stool: How Toilet Posture Affects Your Health."
    YouTube, Squatty Potty, 5 July 2012, www.youtube.com/watch
    ?v=pYcv6odWfTM.
Curious about how much the angle of defecation matters, I purchased a
    Squatty Potty. It's a step stool that changes your posture when you
    are on the pot, setting stool free to slide without any kinks. Not sure
    you should believe their commercial? Bravo. Experiment and come
    to your own conclusion.

"Big Sky Environmental." *Google Maps*, Google, www.google.com/maps
/place/Big+Sky+Environmental,+LLC/@33.6368643,-87.0098161,390
3m/data=!3m1!1e3!4m5!3m4!1s0x8888fbb77b6bdde1:0x39f1b8b7d797
d524!8m2!3d33.644374!4d-87.012398.

Before I visited Big Sky Landfill, I took a flyover, thanks to Google Maps.
With the satellite view, you can zoom in on the landfill cells and
even the neighboring coal-fired power plant. Can you find John's
fishing pond?

"Big Sky Environmental." *Big Sky Environmental*, www.bigskyenv.com/.

Check out the scenery at Big Sky Landfill's website.

"Macroinvertebrate Bioindicators." *Beaver Water District*, 2019, www
.bwdh2o.org/education-outreach/lesson-and-activities/water
-quality/macroinvertebrate-bioindicators/.

It's fun to check the cleanliness of water by looking at the insects
(macroinvertebrates) who can survive in it. Try it once, and you'll be
hooked!

ACKNOWLEDGMENTS

I owe a thank you to just about everyone I know. Whether you shared a story about poop, cast an inquisitive eye at the mention of this topic, laughed (or not) at a story I told, you helped me write this book. For me, writing doesn't wait for me till I sit down at the keyboard. Every story I tell aloud is a draft. Every time I tell it, I am revising.

I want to specifically thank family members who sat through disgusting stories dished out over dinners (the Martins, Montgomerys, Ewings, Taylors, and Leaches), writing friends who coached me through grueling chapters (Darren, Jamie, Jared, Jodi, Joseph, Lisa, Marty, Mary Kay, Nellie, Patty Ann, Rebecca, Tina, plus the July Gals), and hiking buddies (Carolyn, Emily, Janice, and Shannon) who quietly nodded at my ramblings as our soles and souls rambled through wild places.

Then there are all the fabulous folks who gave their time for interviews. People you met, like: Kathleen Black, Dr. Ashli Brown, Dr. Daniella Chusyd, John Click, Gretchen Fowles, Dr. Ari Grinspan, Lauren Guintini, Mayor Heather Hall, Brian Harper, Jennifer Hartman, Dr. Dave Hemprich-Bennett, Dr. Peter Hotez, Hyeon Jeong Kim, Dr. Logan Kistler, Shawn Luker, Ray Madison, Casey McFarland, Dr. Erin McKenney, Dr. Kristen Page and her students, Dr. William Parker, Dr. Joe Roman, Dr. Paul Westerhoff. As well as people you didn't get to meet: Judith Chintz, Wendy Collinson, Carol Henger, Dr. Sarah Karpanty, Alina Kunitskaya (and the whole Astroplastic team), Jasper Lawrence, Dr. Kathleen LoGiudice, Dr. Holly Lutz, Laura Metrione, Cynthia Pollard, Dr. Robert Rockwell,

Dr. Wendy Rosenbek, Dr. Amanda Subalusky, Jeff Summers, Julianne Ubigau, Dr. Bridgett vonHoldt, Dr. Claudia Wultsch, Patricia Yang, and umpteen more. These folks all donated their time to teach me about poo.[1]

There was help from my esteemed agent, Rubin. And then there was that indispensable team at Bloomsbury. From fact-checking to marketing, they helped bring these stories to the world. But most of all, thank you, Susan, for expressing your confidence when I was in too deep to see the story.

---

[1] And they say writing is a solitary profession!

INDEX

Note: The letter n after page numbers refers to footnotes and is followed by the note number. *Italic* page numbers indicate illustrations.

179